PROBLEM POOCH TO PERFECT PET BOOK 1: TROUBLESOME TO TRANQUIL

CAROL CLARK

PROBLEM POOCH TO PERFECT PET

Book 1: Troublesome to Tranquil

Why do dogs do what dogs do?

Sixteen common problems faced by dog owners: at home, with food, and out and about: and how to fix them.

2nd edition © 2022 Carol Clark

ISBN paperback 978-1-915394-06-4

Illustrations by Rob at everyonelovescartoons.com

To Gareth and Himself.
Thanks for everything

CONTENTS

TESTIMONIALS

If a dog could write a book, it would be this one. You would be hard pressed to find a dog problem that's not covered here - apart from the ones that will be covered in the next two books. Overall it causes smiles - and brings hope and challenge!

Alice, dog owner

Not only do you, the writer, want to help make life less troublesome and more tranquil for the owner but the objective is also to make life more tranquil and fulfilling for the pooch. This book will help improve the life of both the owner and the dog. It's also clear that understanding doggy behaviour is important and the book is very clear and helpful in reaching that goal.

As the owner of a dog who had unwanted behaviours, now on the way to being cured thanks to your good self, I was engrossed in the explanations and suggestions and practical tips and steps. I thoroughly enjoyed this book and can't wait for volume 2.

Joanne, dog owner

I have really enjoyed reading the book and found that it has refocused me on our training. I loved the examples and Fred, who has always had dogs, as a recurring theme! It makes the topics relatable and it's also good to know other owners are in the same boat.

Your style is friendly and empathetic, but at the same time knowledgeable and professional. The layout is easy to use and I can see it being the type of "go-to" book that is picked up and consulted regularly. Many congratulations on creating something so enjoyable, useful and entertaining. I genuinely found it an interesting and enjoyable read.

Clare, dog owner

The book captured me from the very first page onwards. The style of writing is so good! It makes me want to read more and more. Exactly the right amount of information without getting boring. Even better than your first two books.

Sandra, dog owner

•   •   •

I'd intended to quickly skim the first bit of your book, but I got sucked in. It's great. Some of the stories made me laugh and I love the cartoons. I don't even have a dog but I love your book, you've done a fantastic job.

Vicky, book-writing guru, Moxie books

I will be giving this book to my clients to save me writing long reports!

Kathy, Smarty Paws Dog Training

WHY THIS BOOK?

Once upon a time I had a problem dog. He was an apprehensive, fearful dog who was scared by his own shadow. He was suspicious of everything. He was reluctant to leave the house to go for walks, hated loud noises and sudden movements, and even had to be taught to play. Worse, he snapped at me often and bit me several times, seemingly out of the blue.

I'd wanted a companion. A doggy friend to walk with and share my life with. To love and enjoy. But that wasn't what I got. I was even scared of him at times.

I was out of my depth with him. I wept with frustration nearly every day because I didn't understand why he was doing these things or how to help him.

It hurts when your dog is not what you expected. You're unhappy, lost and confused.

Your dog is your friend and confidant. He is part of

your family. Perhaps you bought him for companionship, or to fill the empty nest when your children grew up and left home, or to complete your family, or for a whole host of other perfectly valid reasons.

You expect your dog to be perfect just because he's a dog. But no-one has told the dog. He has his own unique mix of behaviours, mannerisms and energy levels. He is the result of his breed and genetics, mixed with his upbringing, experience and environment. Your dog will behave just like a dog. He is not a mini-human. And you may need advice on how to stop the behaviours you don't like.

You may dislike your dog licking his own genitals, urine marking his territory, barking, jumping up, or chewing your fixtures and fittings. You probably hate him pulling you along on walks and get frustrated when he runs off. You may be scared because of his snapping and biting.

But all these things are just normal doggy behaviours.

There's a world of advice out there. Other dog owners are always ready to give advice. Google any question and you'll get a myriad of answers. It's difficult to sort through the countless conflicting suggestions.

I listened to far too many different opinions and made far too many mistakes with my problem dog, but he taught me a huge amount.

He was the main reason I became a dog trainer and behaviourist. That struggle led me into the thirty-odd years of study and gaining practical experience that have resulted in this book series.

If I can prevent just one person having to go through the agony and torment of trying to cope with a dog with a problem behaviour it will all have been worthwhile.

Enjoy.

INTRODUCTION

Jenny wanted the ground to open up beneath her and swallow her whole. She couldn't believe her dog, Shadow, had done it again. And to Jenny's best friend, Susie, too.

Jenny had taken advantage of the brief lull between heavy showers to take Shadow out for a walk. She'd just let Shadow off lead when she spotted Susie sitting on a bench, eating her lunch. Shadow rushed up, jumping at Susie and leaving muddy paw prints all over her new, cream coat. Jenny arrived, panting, and apologised profusely as she gazed in horror at the newly patterned garment. Susie looked at her, tight lipped. Red-faced, Jenny repeatedly apologised as she tried to corral Shadow.

Then, to her utter horror, Shadow grabbed Susie's half-eaten ham sandwich, discarded on the bench when Susie was trying to protect her coat from Shadow's enthusiastic ministrations. At that moment, Jenny hated her dog.

After ten very long minutes, with Susie only slightly pacified by Jenny's promise of picking up the cleaning bill, taking Susie for lunch and buying her a big box of chocolates, Jenny slunk away. Shadow pulled Janet along, dragging her from bush, to tree, to lamppost, but Jenny hardly noticed the discomfort as she brooded on the incident.

When Jenny felt she was far enough away from the crime scene, she let Shadow off lead again to give her aching arm a rest. Shadow decided that the dog he spotted across the park should be his new playmate. Jenny called Shadow back, but he ignored her plaintive cries and ran over to a cavorting spaniel. The two dogs had a great time, running, chasing and play-fighting with each other until both lay down, panting and exhausted. The spaniel owner called his dog away and finally Shadow returned to Jenny.

As they turned for home, Fred's dog, Ludo, a rather overweight Labrador, waddled up to Shadow and stuck his nose into Shadow's unmentionables. Shadow growled, turned, and snapped at Ludo. This was the last straw. Jenny just wanted to be spirited away. For a brief moment, she imagined herself lying on a beach in Barbados.

The daydream was halted abruptly. Fred, who has always had dogs, came huffing up and accused Jenny of having a vicious dog. He proceeded to tell Jenny that she shouldn't have a dog if she can't control it. He informed her that none of his dogs have ever growled. Accompanied by a sternly pointing finger, Fred berated Jenny about how he would stop the behaviour once and for all. Meanwhile, Shadow pawed and whined at Jenny until finally Jenny made a grovelling apology to Fred and crept away.

Are you embarrassed by your naughty dog?

Perhaps you panic when you meet a friend because your dog jumps all over them, or get frustrated because your dog ignores you or runs off when you call him back.

Perhaps you scream in frustration when your dog barks at everything, or maybe you walk your dog before dawn, or in the dead of night, so you don't have to deal with the raving lunatic your dog becomes when he sees another dog.

You long for that ideal dog you knew as a child, who came everywhere with you, seemed to know just what you were thinking, had never had any formal training but was always as good as gold. Even though that dog is likely just as much a myth as you remembering all your childhood summers as being long and sunny. Most dogs are not perfect and they have at least one problem behaviour you'd like to change.

Unless you have a perfect pet, you probably relate to least one of the experiences Jenny suffered and wish there was an easy solution. Perhaps you've searched for advice, but it hasn't helped.

Poor Jenny. Fred, who has always had dogs, is keen to give everyone he meets some advice. He'll appear regularly throughout this book. He's an elderly gentleman who's owned several dogs and has always insisted they do as they're told. As a young man, he attended training classes where he was taught to use choke chains and physical techniques to make his dog do what he wanted. The methods work for him and he wants to pass his experience on to others.

Fred will give advice freely, particularly if your dog has strayed from the ideal: if he has growled, snarled, hid from, lunged at or barked at Fred's own canine companion, in spite of everyone trying to keep away from

Fred and his dog, Ludo, because Ludo runs up to and pesters every dog he sees. No matter. Fred is confident in his opinions – he knows he's right.

All advice is not equal

Dog owners like Fred are usually quick to advise fellow dog owners, even if the advice is not always polite. If you love your dog and enjoy their company, then you'll want others to share the same joy in their canine companions, so you'll happily share your thoughts and ideas.

Unfortunately, enthusiasm and good intentions are not enough and some advice can do more harm than good.

I visited a client recently whose dog is highly reactive to other dogs after a well-meaning stranger told her "just let the dog off lead and let him learn to cope" in a dog park. Bad advice that has caused significant harm to that particular dog which will take a long time to resolve.

All dog owners have their own beliefs about how dogs behave and how to train them.

What Fred says is often neither correct nor useful - but he believes it is.

A sizeable minority of people in the USA believe the world is flat. Many people believe in UFOs and aliens. They believe these things wholeheartedly, despite the evidence that none are true.

We all have our own beliefs about all sorts of things - that going out without a coat and getting wet can cause colds; that there's a monster living in Loch Ness; or that the internet is actually run by pixies.

Every dog owner will have their own set of beliefs. And the thing about beliefs is that - well, we believe them. Sometimes despite overwhelming evidence to the contrary.

Our brains are programmed to filter any advice we receive. We pay the most attention to information that fits with our beliefs and give less, or no, credence to suggestions that don't.

There's so much free advice available nowadays, not just from fellow dog owners.

You only have to type a few words into Google (other search engines are available) to be faced with pages and pages of links to free help from a myriad of sources. Facebook groups abound with posts and comments about every dog problem you can think of.

But there's very little to help you decide what information is trustworthy and what is not. Somehow you have to choose from this pic'n'mix morass of ideas, tips and advice.

At best you might find something that works.

At worst you might make your problem even more annoying, or create another one.

All the freely offered advice from fellow dog owners or on t'internet is overwhelming and often contradictory. You don't know what to do or where to start. You just want practical advice you can apply to your dog and be confident that it'll work.

That's why I've written this book.

This book will help you understand why dogs do the things they do and why they do some things that we find annoying or repugnant. You'll explore unwanted behaviours by reading real stories about owners, the behaviours their dogs showed and how I resolved the issues.

Behavioural Health Warnings (BHWs)

Please note the Behavioural Health Warnings (BHWs) throughout this book. For example:

BHW: Don't blindly accept what Fred, who's always had dogs, says you should or shouldn't do. If you're struggling with your dog's behaviour, please seek proper, professional help.

This book is not meant as a behavioural training textbook, but rather it's a book to help explain why your dog does some of the annoying things they do and to give you hints about solutions you could try.

Do get help if you need it, but make sure your chosen professional is competent to provide it. I've included a chapter at the end of the book on what to look for when searching for qualified help.

BHW: Always get your dog checked over by your vet if he shows any odd behaviour.

Medical causes of behavioural problems are quite common and have caught us all out. My caseload contains a few cases each year where the cause of the unwanted behaviour turns out to be a physical problem or illness.

How to use this book

There are two sections in this book. The first section looks at some behavioural basics - why dogs do what they do, exploding the dominance myth, and explaining why neutering is not a panacea for all behavioural ills. This section finishes by explaining the two options for changing your dog's behaviour and outlines my three-step plan to success.

In the second section I look at sixteen common behaviour problems. These include six common problems in the home, six worries related to food and feeding, and finally the four most common issues you'll face outside your home.

Using anonymised case studies from my extensive portfolio, I explain the possible reasons why your dog might have chosen to perform that particular behaviour, then give you a range of tips you can try to change that unwanted behaviour in your own dog.

Feel free to jump to the chapters you want to know more about, or read the book right through, whatever works for you.

If you're struggling with trying to address a particular unwanted behaviour in your pooch, are keen to find out what works and are committed to putting time and effort into changing things, then read on.

I hope this book will help you turn life with your dog from troublesome to tranquil.

Let's start by delving into the basics of dog behaviour in part 1.

PART I

WHAT IS GOOD BEHAVIOUR ANYWAY?

Susan felt so proud of Bruno. She'd taken him on his usual walk to the park and they'd met a young family who wanted to pet him. Bruno stood beautifully, wagging his tail, while the two young children stroked him. He sniffed one child's hand then gave it a quick lick, which made the child giggle, and everyone walked on with smiles on their faces. As she walked home, Bruno ignored a discarded portion of chips on the path and walked straight past Toto, the Terrible Terrier, who was hurling himself at his (luckily substantial) fence, frantically barking his heart out.

Noticing behaviour

Walks like this make you feel proud of your well-behaved dog. But so often you just don't notice what your dog is doing - until he does something you don't like.

We don't celebrate nearly enough all the wonderful things in life that we see, do and feel. We don't focus enough on nature's beauty, or spend enough time dwelling on the pleasure of doing something nice for a friend, or just enjoying watching children (or dogs) playing, or rejoice in our own health and well-being when we're feeling good.

Humans are hard-wired to focus on problems. We worry for ages about the things in our lives that concern or upset us. And most of them aren't really important. Is my neighbour looking disapprovingly over the fence because our garden is messy? Should I wear my best dress or a suit to go to dinner with work colleagues? I've accepted my friend's party invitation but I don't really want to go, what shall I do?

You easily get distressed by the nasty things people say and rehash the conversation repeatedly, worrying at it like a dog with a bone.

It's actually part of our brain set-up. Focusing on problems and dangers gave us a significant survival benefit in the days when we were hunter-gatherers. But perhaps it's not as useful now. It stops you from developing to your full potential and holds you back from trying things that feel scary.

Although you don't have to fight mammoths, leopards or lions nowadays, your brain is still wired to focus on negatives rather than positives. And that's what happens when it comes to your pet dog too.

You're far more likely to focus on your dog when he does something bad; when he barks, or chews your favourite pair of shoes, or steals food from the counter, or pees up the curtain. But you don't notice him when he's good, sitting or lying down quietly, or chewing his bone.

Dogs learn quickly that misbehaving gets them attention. Many dogs will bark, jump up, steal, chew, or run away with your mobile phone, simply to get you to react and acknowledge their existence.

Set aside half an hour today and just watch your pooch. Ask yourself simply "is he being good or bad?" You'll be amazed to find that he's being good, doing things you're happy with, 85-90% (at least) of the time.

What is good or bad behaviour?

Dogs are social animals who thrive on attention and social interaction. They have no concept of good or bad. Dogs behave the way they do simply because that's the way dogs behave. They chew, bark, growl, pull on lead or run away because that's the way their brains tell them to react or behave - and often how we've allowed, or inadvertently trained, our dogs to behave.

Using the words "good" or "bad" isn't really helpful. There is no universal definition of what constitutes good or bad behaviour, although there's some common consensus on certain behaviours. Nobody wants their dog to steal food, or enjoys returning to a trail of destruction when they've left their pooch alone in the house, or likes their dog running off if the door is left slightly ajar, or prefers their dog to bark all the time.

"Good" behaviour is normal dog behaviour that we

humans consider to be acceptable, appropriate or desirable. Equally, "bad" behaviour is simply normal dog behaviour that we consider to be unacceptable, inappropriate or undesirable.

Pulling on lead, not coming when called, food stealing, digging, jumping up, sniffing, running over to other dogs, play-fighting, pawing, whining – you may see any or all of these as problem behaviours.

All of these are also normal behaviours that ordinary dogs do. Which leads us to an important truth:

Whether a behaviour is seen as a problem or not depends on your perspective as the owner.

A better term than "problem behaviour" is "unwanted behaviour" – after all, a farmer who wants to rid his yard of rats will encourage his terrier to dig them out and kill them; the gundog handler wants his spaniel to delve deep into the undergrowth to flush birds out; the security guard supports his German Shepherd or Rottweiler barking and lunging at people.

Are dogs Machiavellian?

Do you feel that your dog is doing things to spite or annoy you? He isn't. He's just being a dog. Dogs are basically simple creatures. They do the stuff that works for them.

They don't lie in bed at night planning to take over your world.

They don't chew your best pair of slippers because they're annoyed you wouldn't let them chase next door's cat.

They don't poo on your new carpet because they're miffed you left them home alone.

Dogs do the things that get them what they want or make them feel good. If what your dog does results in something he likes or finds pleasant, he'll do it more - and more.

If stealing a sock means you chase them, they'll keep stealing socks.

If jumping up gets them the attention they want, they'll jump up again and again.

If pulling on lead gets them where they want to go quicker, they'll pull on lead.

If running off to play with another dog is more fun, they won't come back.

Dogs do the things that get the result the dog wants. Dogs don't have any morals. They don't understand the concept of behaviours being inherently good or bad, they just do the things that make them feel good or that help them avoid something that makes them feel uncomfortable.

If Jess starts biting you when playing and you immediately stop playing and ignore her, she'll decide that biting people is not a good thing.

If Bonzo gets a biscuit every time he sits and gazes at you with those big, sad eyes, he'll decide that sitting gazing at you is a good thing.

If Simba loves playing with other dogs, he'll run up to other dogs when off lead.

If Roxy jumps up on the kitchen counter and finds a

tasty morsel to snaffle, she'll keep doing it in case there's food there again.

If Rex barks and you shout at him to shut up, he'll learn that barking works to get your attention.

None of these behaviours are seen as bad by the dog of course - they're normal dog behaviours. But to you they're unwanted behaviours.

Some behaviours, even if not especially wanted, you might see as acceptable. Chihuahua owners usually don't mind if their pooch pulls on lead - but German Shepherd owners usually do. Shih Tzu owners may not mind if their dog jumps on the furniture - but St Bernard owners often do. A hunter will actively encourage his gundog to flush birds out from the undergrowth - but a pet owner will get frazzled if their dog spends his time chasing birds in the park.

Some collie owners may enjoy their dog madly running circles round them, or obsessively chasing balls, while others see a problem they need to deal with. Some beagle owners might watch with pride as their hound sets off after a scent, while others wish their dog would always come back when they called.

A few owners seem to think that pets should train themselves. They see perfect dogs in the media, the movies and on the street and seem to believe that good behaviour just happens. The truth is, well-behaved dogs are the result of their owners putting in a lot of time and effort, attending (good) dog training classes and bucket-loads of hard work.

You need to teach your dog what behaviours are acceptable to you and what aren't.

Why does it matter?

Fred, who has always had dogs, is quite happy to allow his dog to run up to other dogs. After all, his dog is friendly, most of the time. Surely it doesn't really matter - after all, dogs will be dogs.

Well, Fred, it does matter how your dog behaves. If your dog scares another dog by running up, that other dog might react by growling, snarling or snapping. Which might be the start of that dog growling and snapping at any other dog it then sees.

BHW: Never, ever, allow your dog to run up to another dog. Never. Ever.

The biggest killer of young dogs in the UK is behaviour problems.

And the bitter truth is that the majority of these problems can be prevented by good socialisation and many of the rest can be helped through good behavioural training.

A 2015 survey by the British Veterinary Association (BVA) showed that 98 per cent of vets have been asked to euthanise healthy pets, with 53 per cent of vets saying that this isn't a rare occurrence.

In nearly every case "bad behaviour" by the pet was the reason for the euthanasia request.

Dogs should not pay the price for their human's lack of knowledge.

When someone's untrained cuddly puppy grows up and starts becoming aggressive and pushy at home, or tears the place apart when they leave the house, or starts attacking other pets, or won't toilet outside, or starts barking and annoying the neighbours while they're at work, they may see euthanasia of that 'problem' dog as a quick fix: problem solved.

This is just not acceptable.

Pets can be, and are, euthanised for severe behavioural issues such as aggression causing damage to others, however, euthanasia for anything else must be a last resort.

You've probably heard these common excuses for unwanted behaviour - "it's because he's a (insert breed here)", or "She's a rescue dog, so....", and the classic "He's just being dominant."

Using your dog's breed, personality, or where you got him from as an excuse for you not training him is just a smokescreen. All dogs need training and all dogs will respond to good training methods. That's not to say it's always easy, it isn't.

Perhaps you recognise that your dog is just not the right dog for you or your lifestyle. Rehoming might be one option, but the impact on your family of giving your pet up might be too much.

Getting expert help could be the answer. There are so many other options to help you work through problems, such as dog training classes, veterinary advice, and consultation and assistance from a competent behaviourist.

If you're struggling with your dog's unwanted behaviours, hopefully you'll find some help in this book (and the following volumes), but please, please, think about seeking competent, professional help, too.

Summary

- Dogs do the things that work for them - that make them feel good or help them avoid something that makes them feel uncomfortable
- Behaviours are not inherently "good" or "bad" - it's your view as an owner that determines whether behaviours are acceptable and wanted, or not
- The biggest killer of young, healthy dogs is behaviour problems
- If you're struggling with your dog's behaviour, please seek expert help

We'll explode the dominance myth once and for all in the next chapter.

1

IS MY DOG BEING DOMINANT?

Simon was panicking. He was going to be late for work - again. Murphy was running up and down the beach, sniffing at rocks, throwing seaweed up in the air then worrying it as he caught it again, oblivious to Simon's distress and to his increasingly panicked pleas for him to "come HERE."

Finally, Simon managed to grab him as he ran past and put his lead on. As he turned to set off as fast as he could towards his car, he bumped into Fred, who has always had dogs, and who had seen everything. "Your dog's being dominant" said Fred. "He thinks he's the boss and so he's doing what he wants. You need to be the pack leader and be firm with him."

What is the Dominance Theory?

The dominance theory of dog ownership held centre stage around 30-40 years ago. The theory basically went as follows: Dogs are descended from wolves and wolves form packs with an alpha leader. Therefore dogs are born wanting to be a pack leader and they look for opportunities to dominate humans.

Wrong.

It all started when an animal behaviourist, Rudolph Schenkel, researched two captive wolf packs in a Swiss zoo in the late 1940s. He identified two primary wolves in a pack: a male 'lead wolf' and a female lead 'bitch'. He described them as 'first in the pack group' and noted that rivalries between wolves in the pack were subdued by these lead wolves. Thus the idea of the alpha leader was born.

Much of Schenkel's work compared wolves and domestic dogs and the implication was clear: wolves live in packs in which individual members vie for dominance and therefore dogs, their domestic brethren, must be similar.

Further research on captive wolves by wildlife biologist David Mech in the 1960s initially corroborated these findings and his hit 1970 book *The Wolf: The ecology and behaviour of an endangered species* promoted the idea of the alpha wolf. (It remains a popular book, much to his chagrin, today.)

Research continued by Mech and others over the next couple of decades, but now they focused on wolves in the wild. In 1999, Mech published a paper (*Alpha Status, Dominance and Division of Labor in Wolf Packs*) which was the turning point in understanding the true structure of wolf packs.

"The concept of the alpha wolf as a 'top dog' ruling a

group of similar-aged compatriots is particularly misleading," Mech wrote. He found that wolves live in families. The pack consists of two parents along with their younger cubs. As the wolf offspring grow up they are dispersed from the family group, meet up with other dispersed wolves, have cubs, and form packs (families) of their own.

Wolves don't have an innate sense of rank; they are not born leaders or born followers. The 'alphas' are simply what we would call in any other social group 'parents'.

Unfortunately, the idea of the 'alpha' wolf took hold in the world of dog training in the second half of the 20th century and dominance reduction training methods were rife. I was taught this way when I got my first dog. So was Fred.

If dogs misbehaved, it was assumed they were trying to be 'dominant' and trainers used forceful methods to 'train' the dog until it gave in. Trainers taught owners to use unpleasant and harmful training methods such as using choke chains to yank their dogs to heel beside them, or, worse, employ the so-called 'alpha rolls' which involved holding a dog down on its back until it 'submitted'.

BHW: *Some TV shows still advocate physical ways to 'subdue' your dog. These methods are downright dangerous.*

Why using dominance reduction methods matters

Many other dominance theory based ideas are still around today. You've probably seen or heard these: Don't let your dog walk through the door before you do. Don't let her win a game of tug. Don't let him eat before you do.

These methods and rules don't teach your dog anything good. Instead, you'll risk your dog becoming fearful of you and not trusting you, which in turn can create a whole range of difficult behaviour problems.

BHW: Pack leader rules and 'rank reduction' methods can damage your relationship with your dog

Until your dog develops opposable thumbs, or opens his own bank account, you're the boss in your relationship. He can choose which toy to play with - but you buy the toys. You control his food, where he sleeps, when he goes out and where, and who he meets and plays with. In the same way as you're the parent (boss) to your children when they're young - well, I think I was - most of the time, anyway.

You don't need to be a 'pack leader'. But you do need to help your dog by showing leadership and helping him make the right choices about how to behave. Just as you would as a parent to your child.

Let's once and for all forget about applying erroneous wolf behaviour findings to how we raise and train our dogs. Rather than worrying about your dog's status in your family and whether he's trying to dominate you and take over the world, let's celebrate his wonderful doggy traits and talents and use these characteristics to help and train him to be a good family member.

Summary

- The idea of the alpha wolf is incorrect
- Dogs are not trying to dominate us
- Training methods based on being a "pack leader" are outdated and potentially dangerous

While we're on a roll exploding a few myths, in the next chapter you'll find out why neutering is not a panacea for unwanted behaviour.

2

WILL NEUTERING IMPROVE MY DOG'S BEHAVIOUR?

On a glorious summer's day, Simon was out walking his dog, Murphy. As they strolled across the park, Fred approached with his dog, Ludo. Ludo sniffed at Murphy then stalked round and placed his paw over Murphy's neck. Murphy growled and snapped at Ludo and the two dogs squared up. As the men pulled their dogs apart, Fred, who's always had dogs, was offended. "Your dog should have his balls off," he told Simon, "That'd stop him being so aggressive." Simon harrumphed and strode off before he said something he'd regret. He had no intention of neutering Murphy. He would keep clear of Fred and Ludo in future.

It's a real conundrum for many owners - should I neuter or not?

Many vets recommend early neutering, at or before 6 months of age. Rescue organisations push to castrate and spay all their dogs, even puppies. There's a real problem with the UK having too many dogs needing rehoming and all rescue organisations are creaking at the seams. Neutering seems a sensible option to help.

Unfortunately, there is no evidence anywhere in the world that a neutering programme does anything to reduce the number of unwanted dogs. (Neither does dog licensing or microchipping, incidentally).

In general, neutering is a good thing. There's some recent evidence that neutered dogs live slightly longer. It also takes away the risk of you ending up with a surprise present of unwanted puppies and the stress of having to find them good homes.

BHW: Raising a litter of puppies properly is very time consuming and expensive if done correctly – it certainly isn't a way to make an easy buck.

There's a fair amount of information about the health impacts of neutering, but not much about the behavioural effects, although further studies are underway. Let's explore what we know from the evidence to date.

Should I spay my bitch?

For bitches, there is good evidence to support spaying.

The risk of breast cancer is significantly reduced if your bitch is spayed before 2½ years of age. A full spay (taking out the uterus and ovaries) eliminates the risk of pyometra (pus in the uterus) and uterine, cervical or ovarian cancer. Laparoscopic (keyhole) spaying, where only the ovaries are removed, is now becoming routine in many areas.

Reasons for not spaying are: it's irreversible; there's a small risk (4-20%) of urinary incontinence in later life (if your bitch leaks urine, such as with excitement peeing, please do not spay until that has stopped), and it can increase the risk of hypothyroidism and obesity. There are also risks from the anaesthetic.

On the behaviour side, spaying may reduce learning ability slightly. It may also cause an increase in 'masculinised' behaviours such as urine marking and raised leg urination.

On balance, the health benefits of spaying female dogs exceed the possible health problems. When to spay is your choice, but probably from a minimum of six months of age onwards.

Many vets now recommend spaying before the first season, but there are some good reasons for delaying it until your dog has had one season – you can then be sure your dog has gone through puberty, which is important for bone and joint health and possibly has positive behavioural effects, too.

Should I neuter my dog?

For male dogs, the decision whether to neuter or not is more difficult.

Health wise, castration can reduce some prostate problems in later life. It eliminates testicular tumours - but prostatic tumours can still occur. If done before one year of age it can significantly increase the risk of bone cancer in some breeds. It can also increase the risk of hypothyroidism, doggy dementia and obesity.

Overall, no compelling case can be made for neutering

most male dogs in order to prevent future health problems - but socially it's probably a good thing to do. When to do it is your choice, but I strongly suggest this is not before your dog starts to cock his leg when urinating and preferably not until at least 12 months of age, to allow brain and physical maturation from the testosterone surge of puberty and to reduce the bone cancer risk.

Does neutering help with unwanted behaviours?

Neutering can reduce sexually initiated behaviours, such as humping or urine marking, and it may reduce the risk of your dog roaming. It may also be beneficial if your dog has sexual frustration. But all of these behaviours may occur for other reasons, in which case neutering will have no impact.

You may be considering neutering because your dog is crazy, always running around, destroying your home, jumping up on everyone and generally over-the-top. Forget the idea. It won't work.

BHW: Neutering has absolutely no impact on hyperactive behaviour. Nada. None.

Some vets will recommend neutering for dogs that show aggression, but it can make aggression worse, especially if the aggressive behaviour is related to fear or anxiety. Spaying may reduce reactivity and aggression in bitches - but only if this behaviour occurs solely when the bitch is in season.

Early neutering at around the vet recommended age of six months in dogs seems to increase the risk of inviting aggression from other dogs and may increase non-season related reactivity and aggression in bitches.

So what's the conclusion from all this?

In a nutshell, there are good health and reproductive reasons to neuter, but there's no evidence it helps with non-sexual unwanted behaviours.

Summary

- Spaying bitches provides health benefits
- Sexually driven and sexually related unwanted behaviours may be helped by neutering
- Aggression problems may worsen after neutering, especially if they're fear based
- Neutering has no effect on hyperactivity

If neutering's not the answer to most unwanted behaviours, what is?

We'll talk about how you can change unwanted behaviours in the next chapter.

3

HOW CAN I CHANGE MY DOG'S
UNWANTED BEHAVIOUR?

C lare was fed up with Max. He just wouldn't listen to
her at all. She knew he was still just a puppy at six
months old, but his charging round the house,
stealing and chewing toys, socks and shoes, jumping up at the
children when they were playing in the garden and tripping her
up by getting under her feet all the time, was getting her down.
She was enjoying the training classes, but the things they taught
her didn't help her change how Max behaved at home. She was
really struggling. At her training class, Fred, who's always had
dogs, told her she was too soft and she should try tapping Max
on his nose or shouting when he tried to steal something and
chasing him away with a broom if he chased the children.

If you've experienced a new puppy you'll be nodding
and empathising with Clare.

It's really tiring dealing with a puppy.

Just when you've sorted the house training and
stopped the nipping and biting, your sweet, cute little

bundle of fluff morphs into a gangly, obnoxious teenager. His puppy behaviours aren't so funny anymore. They're annoying, frustrating - and sometimes expensive.

It's all too easy to ignore your dog's bad behaviour.

We all have tough times and it's easy to wallow in a vat of self-pity, but pacing around with a hand on your fevered brow saying "woe is me, I've got the worst puppy in the world," or simply ignoring the problem, crossing your fingers and hoping it will improve of its own accord, is pointless.

The bad news first - there are no magic bullets. If you're honest, you probably just want someone to wave a magic wand and make all your problems go away. I often want that. For all sorts of things. But it only happens in fairy tales.

Forget that idea.

The good news is that nearly all unwanted behaviours can be stopped, changed, or improved significantly.

But it takes work - sometimes a LOT of work. If you're not prepared to put the work in, then you might as well stop reading now. This book won't help you.

BHW: If you do nothing, the behaviour will almost certainly get worse - behaviours rarely stay the same. So you need to change something.

At my heaviest I feel like a supertanker - large, heavy and difficult to manoeuvre. And age doesn't help. Trying to lose weight is just like turning a supertanker round. You have to do it slowly and it takes a long, long time.

I struggle with losing weight and I know it's because I have some bad eating habits, including eating sugary starchy foods when I'm bored or upset, and liking chocolate too much. One of my bad habits is to reach for a biscuit with my final evening coffee (a chocolate biscuit of course - I'm partial to a KitKat).

To lose weight I have to change those habits.

Sometimes habits can be even more sneaky and set themselves up without us realising.

When you're eating a biscuit, your dog comes up and sits in front of you, gazing at you with those pleading doggy eyes. You give him a piece, telling yourself you're rewarding his attention on you - but you're actually setting up a begging habit.

When your dog steals your slipper and you yell at him and run after him to get it back, he'll enjoy the chase game - and you're setting up a stealing habit.

When your dog lunges forward on lead you stop, call him back and give him a treat beside you. But he doesn't learn to stop pulling and you don't know why. Surely you're teaching him to be at your side by giving him a treat there? Well, no - you've set up a habit. Your dog has learnt to pull, then wait for you to call before coming back for a treat.

If your dog is doing something you don't want him to do, then something has to change.

It's YOU that needs to make that change - your dog is quite happy with the status quo. And it's easiest to make that change before the behaviour becomes a habit.

Why does my dog do what he does?

Dogs do the things that either make them feel good or help them avoid something that makes them feel uncomfortable. (Remember - behaviours are only unwanted when we deem them to be.)

If something makes your dog feel good, we call that thing a reward. A reward can be all sorts of things - comfort (lying on the settee), the act of chewing (anything - including your best shoes), yummy food to eat (especially when stolen), attention from us (particularly when we're busy with something else), or satisfying a chase instinct (especially when the something chased is alive).

Stealing socks and shoes gets your attention and gives your dog his reward as you chase him to try and retrieve the item. Telling your dog off can be a reward to your dog - from the attention you're giving him. Perhaps your dog's reward is the endorphin release he gets from running around after your children, or from jumping up at guests. Or perhaps his reward for running out into the garden when the children are playing is to avoid being shut up in the house.

Here's another vitally important point:

Whether or not something is a reward depends on how _your dog_ perceives it, not your view of it.

You may think your patting his head is rewarding - but he may dislike that type of touch. You may think giving him a piece of kibble is a reward - but your dog may not be hungry. You may think offering him his tug toy is a reward

- but he may prefer to go and sniff the lamp post over there.

Whether something is seen by your dog as rewarding or not depends on what the reward is, when and where it is given, whether there's something more enticing available, and what state your dog is in at that moment.

If your dog is performing a particular behaviour then he is somehow getting a reward for doing it.

Working out what the precise reward is for that particular dog in that distinct situation is key to understanding why your dog does the behaviour - and essential when finding ways to change unwanted behaviours.

Should I use force to make him do what I want?

Fred, who's always had dogs, suggested forceful methods to change Max's behaviour - to punish Max when he did something Clare didn't want. Most people have heard of, read, or seen this sort of advice - tap your dog on the nose when he barks; hit him with a rolled up newspaper when he toilets in the house; or squirt him with water if he's naughty.

You'll hear these sorts of things from lots of people - it sounds like normal, good advice.

Beware.

There are six big problems with using forceful techniques:

1) Punishment is an easy option for humans. It requires less brain power to react to your dogs unwanted

behaviour than to think about why your dog is doing it and how you could proactively prevent him doing it instead. It's the lazy option.

2) You need to be sure what you do is punishing to your dog. A squirt of water may indeed be unpleasant for some dogs, but others will love it and it's a reward for them.

3) Punishment may reduce the behaviour, but only temporarily. Especially when it's not linked with rewarding acceptable behaviour.

4) It might tell your dog what he shouldn't be doing, but it gives him no help at all to teach him what he should do instead.

5) Punishment will definitely harm your relationship with your dog.

6) Finally, effective punishment has to be used consistently and timed perfectly. Most of us can't manage that.

BHW: *Punishment just doesn't work. There are much better options.*

If you punish your dog for toileting on your rug, he might decide to hide his eliminations behind the curtain or sofa instead.

If you punish your dog for raiding your bin, he'll just make sure you're not around next time he wants to do it.

If you punish your dog for not coming back immediately when you call, he'll be even less likely to come in future.

Your dog is not looking guilty when you come home to find your new Jimmy Choos destroyed, or a mess on the carpet. Dogs will 'look guilty' if scolded or when you are cross, whether they've done something or not. The main reason for your dog 'looking guilty' when you return is *your* behaviour, not anything your dog has or hasn't done. In other words, your behaviour as an owner and your history of scolding or reprimands is what makes your dog 'look guilty'.

If punishment doesn't work, what can I do?

First, identify what reward(s), or benefit(s), your dog is getting when they do the behaviour. The reward may be from you, or it may be from the situation or the environment.

Does he get your attention by barking?

Does she get you to move faster if she pulls on the lead?

Does he get a fuss from you when he pushes at your hand?

Do other dogs keep away when she barks at them?

Does he get to eat the food he steals from the kitchen counter?

My assistants were laughing at me recently. I'd subconsciously been trained by my current dog, Gus. I was feeding him random bits of food for staying quietly by my side while I was teaching a class. He started putting his foot on top of mine and when he did, I fed him. He'd trained me to give him food whenever he wanted, by putting his foot on mine. He'd set his own reward criteria.

Work out what reward your dog is getting.

Once you've identified the reward(s) your dog is getting for the unwanted behaviour, you need a plan.

Your plan can be cunning as a fox or may just involve a simple change in routine.

To change your dogs unwanted behaviour, you have two options:

OPTION 1: Teach the dog to do something else instead (for which he gets at least an equivalent reward)

Doing something else instead can be teaching your dog to go to bed instead of begging for food at the dinner table. Or to lie quietly at your side when you go around to your friend's house instead of destroying her garden. Or to go into his crate to eat a yummy Kong instead of jumping at the children when they're playing.

OPTION 2: Stop the reward(s) the dog is getting for the behaviour.

Stopping the rewards can include removing the kitchen bin to stop bin raiding. Or putting food away to stop your dog stealing it from the kitchen counter. Or, in my case, not giving a treat when Gus puts his paw on my foot.

Simple, yes? Yes - and no.

Dog training is indeed simple - but it's not necessarily easy. Think of that old saying: How do you eat an elephant? The answer: in bite sized chunks. To achieve anything in life you need to focus on the small steps and break all the big stuff down into smaller , achievable pieces.

I'll be doing that with the sixteen unwanted behaviours covered in this book. But in the meantime, here's my basic three step plan for changing your dogs unwanted behaviour:

STEP 1: Decide which of the two options above you're going to use for each unwanted behaviour. With Max, Clare could teach him to 'leave' to stop him stealing shoes and socks and she could teach him 'stay' to keep him from getting under her feet (option 1). Or she could use baby gates or other barriers to stop him charging round the house and she could shut him in when the children were running around the garden (option 2).

Keep your plan as simple as possible.

STEP 2: Put your plan into action, one thing at a time. Don't try to do everything at once. Pick the unwanted behaviour you like least to address first. Or pick the one that seems easiest to do. Your choice.

Use a reward your dog loves to teach him what you want him to do instead. Clare decided to give Max a filled Kong in the utility room while the children were out playing. Simple and effective. Once you've dealt with that problem, move on to the next bit of your plan and do that one. One thing at a time. Keep it simple.

STEP 3: Make sure everyone in the family knows what the plan is and agrees to help, so everyone does the same thing. Consistency is key. It's no good deciding you don't want your dog on the furniture if the children encourage him up there for a cuddle each evening. It's no good trying to teach your dog to settle on his bed at dinner time if your husband surreptitiously feeds him under the table.

Tell your family and friends what you want to do.

Engage their help. Write it down. Put key messages up on the fridge so everyone sees them regularly.

Keep it clear and simple.

Summary

- Behaviour never stays the same - your dog will get better at it with practice. If you don't change something the behaviour will get worse
- There are two ways to change an unwanted behaviour: either teach your dog to do something else instead, or stop your dog getting the reward for it
- You need a simple, achievable, 3-step action plan that everyone will follow

I'll talk about 16 common unwanted behaviours and what you can do about them in the second part of this book. You can use that information to help you make your cunning plan.

PART II

BEFORE YOU READ ON...

Your idea of your Perfect Pet may be different to mine. How you want your dog to behave will be based on your individual desires - you want a dog you can live in harmony with and enjoy each other's company.

The following chapters will help you understand and know what to do to change the things your dog does that spoil that dream.

No dog is perfect - just like no human is perfect. Dogs are dogs and will behave like dogs - jumping up, pulling on lead, stealing and begging for food, chewing things, running off, barking, growling - the list of unwanted behaviours is huge.

Whether you see any of these things as unwanted depends on so many other factors - your lifestyle, your family, where you live, your beliefs and your experiences. There are so many permutations.

- If you're caring for a frail elderly relative you may be particularly concerned about stopping your dog jumping up.

- If you have young children you may need to stop your dog stealing food from their plates.

- If you have arthritis you may be desperate to stop your dog pulling on lead.

- If you've just bought a new dining room suite you may be frantic to prevent your dog chewing.

- If you live in the country you may be terrified of your dog running off and worrying sheep.

The following chapters cover sixteen common unwanted behaviours seen regularly in pet dogs. Using real stories and case histories from my files, each chapter describes the problem, explains why the dog might be doing it and offers tips for you to try at home to combat these unwanted behaviours.

There's never one simple reason why a dog will do any particular behaviour.

My answer to any 'why does my dog?' question is always "it depends". In each chapter I'll describe the range of possible reasons which could apply to your dog. You'll have to do the detailed detective work, though.

All the stories and examples are real, though my client's and their dog's names have been changed for anonymity. My own dog, Gus, features as well as my husband, known as Himself to my regular email and blog followers.

This book can help you turn your life with your dog from troublesome to tranquil.

But please do seek professional help if you're struggling - the final chapter in the book will help you with that.

A quick note: For ease of reading, I use 'him' and 'her' randomly when referring to dogs throughout the book. Just because I hate the use of 'him/her' - and I won't even countenance 'it'.

Ok. Off we go. We'll start with those annoying behaviours your dog might do at home. Let's jump right in and talk about – jumping up.

4

HOW CAN I STOP MY DOG JUMPING UP?

On holiday with my relatives and their two dogs last year, I was lying snoozing in bed, dreaming of Daniel Craig emerging from the sea, all dripping and glistening... oops, enough of that! - when the door shot open and two large, brown vizslas crashed into the bedroom. Immediately they realised I was at a significant disadvantage, lying wrapped in my duvet, with no glasses on and struggling to understand what was happening. Me asleep + two dogs awake = no contest. Cyril leapt up, stuffed his nose into my face and proceeded to lick me. One swipe up the face and my nose, cheeks and eyes were glistening with doggy drool. As I tried to fight him off, Norman took advantage of the distraction by jumping on the bed and attacked my neck with big sloppy kisses from behind.

I tried reason - no good. Cyril and Norman don't understand many cue words and they weren't in a mood to react even if they'd understood my muffled shrieks. I tried gently restraining *them - useless. My two arms versus two big, wriggly, brown masses of muscle was not even a starter. So I used the underhand tactic of wriggling down the bed and wrapping myself in the duvet. They burrowed after me for a short while but then gave up and went off after easier prey. (And found it, judging by the screams and shouts from my brother-in-law in the next room.)*

Why do dogs jump up?

Jumping up is one of the most common problems you might need help with. Why do so many dogs jump up at people?

It depends.

Puppies learn to jump up at their mother's mouth when they're being weaned, to get the food she brings back to them. Dogs carry this behaviour on into their adult lives, licking each other's mouths and faces as a greeting. Human mouths are further off the ground, so our canine friends jump up to reach our mouths and faces to lick us when they want to greet us.

Puppies quickly learn to get attention by jumping up. It can be difficult to resist that cuddly bundle of fur scrabbling at your legs, and you'll bend down and pick the puppy up, or give it a fuss.

You might see jumping up as cute and sweet when your puppy is tiny - but it's a different kettle of fish when your 6 stone Labrador does it. Perhaps you keep rewarding this behaviour with the attention you give: telling your dog to "get off" and pushing him down will never cure jumping up - in fact it usually makes it worse.

As does inconsistency. Family members or friends can easily sabotage your training. Beware the Comment of Calamity: "I don't mind him jumping up," from your subverting acquaintance.

Rough housing with the dog will encourage jumping up (and often biting, too). The male of our species is often the main instigator of this indiscipline. There were three red faces at my recent puppy party as the men sheepishly admitted that was exactly what they did.

There can be several other reasons for jumping up;

- some dogs will jump up to push you away when they don't want you to come close to them

- some may jump up because they want to protect something they see as valuable

- some dogs jump up from anxiety or fear, to keep you away and protect themselves

- your dog may jump up to tell you he's physically uncomfortable because he needs to go out to eliminate.

You can tell whether your dog wants interaction or not by *how* they jump up. A jump where the dog places his paws gently on your body and controls his own body weight tells you the dog wants your attention and fuss. Conversely, if your dog jumps up and nearly pushes you over with the weight and force behind his paws, he may be saying he's not completely happy about the potential interaction - the jumping up is designed to get him some space. Or he may just be an untrained, unruly dog of course.

Boisterous, danger-of-knocking-you-over jumping up can be inadvertently trained if your dog is unsure about how you may react. The usual cause of this is inconsistency. He may be uncertain about whether you're going to be happy to greet him or whether you're going to tell him off for jumping up.

Ask yourself, are you being unclear with your dog?

Do you allow your dog to jump up when you're relaxing in your casual clothes, but you get cross with him when you're dressed smartly for work?

Are you happy for your dog to jump up at you when you come in, but you don't want him to jump up at visitors?

You need to decide from the start whether you want your dog jumping up at you or others, or not. And you have to be consistent.

How can I stop my dog jumping up?

The best way to stop jumping up is to teach your dog to do something else - either to sit when being greeted, or simply to keep all four paws on the floor.

If you reward the jumping up your dog will just get better and better at it.

It's unfair on the dog to allow him to jump up sometimes but tell him off at other times.

Jumping up is inherently rewarding to your dog anyway, so he'll become confused if you allow him to jump up sometimes but scold him at other times.

We dog trainers call that 'random reinforcement'. It's extremely powerful in training and it heavily encourages the behaviour it's given for - so don't let it apply to jumping up, or guess what? Your dog will keep on jumping up.

When your puppy is small and cute, jumping up and licking your face can seem adorable and fun – "My puppy loves me!" so we allow it (and enjoy it).

But what dogs practice they get good at. Once the puppy grows and becomes a gangly teenager, jumping up and licking faces are usually seen as a problem.

You may love the puppy kisses and licks you get, but whenever he jumps up and you give him cuddles and fuss him, you're encouraging that behaviour.

If you want kisses from your dog (and there's nothing wrong with that), it's best to get down to him instead of him jumping up at you.

BHW: *If you don't want your puppy to jump up when he grows bigger, then don't allow it when he's a young puppy.*

The best rule to have is that four paws should be on the floor for your dog to get any attention from you. Train this from the moment you get your puppy.

Use the following training tips to help you do the right things.

Tip 1: Right from the start, don't let your puppy practice jumping up. Instead, get down to her level to play with her and fuss her.

Tip 2: Keep toys low down, parallel to the floor, when playing with her.

Greeting your dog

You're most likely to encourage jumping up when you come back home. Let's face it, who isn't glad to see their dog when they come home?

You may get a kick out of your dog jumping all over you when you come in from work, because she's so pleased to see you (and you're so pleased to see her). "Hello Milly," you say, "I've had a rotten day at work. Give mummy a cuddle." And both of you enjoy the experience of your dog jumping up; after all, you're stiff, tired and fed up from sitting in your office all day, so having this unconditional love poured out as you come in is highly gratifying. Not to mention it's easier on your tired body for your dog to come up to your level instead of you having to bend down to her.

It's theoretically possible for your dog to learn that it's OK to jump on you but it's not OK to jump on visitors, but I don't recommend this approach.

If your dog is allowed to jump up sometimes, or on some people, there is a high risk that your dog will try to jump up on other people when you (and they) don't want her to.

BHW: Inconsistency in training is the most common cause of unwanted behaviours continuing.

Perhaps you actively encourage the behaviour. "But I'm not encouraging it", you say, "I don't praise her for jumping up." You're probably encouraging it without realising. It's normal human behaviour to tell your dog off ("stop it, get down") or to push her away when she jumps up. Unfortunately, both of these responses actually REWARD the jumping up and make it more likely to happen again.

Instead, try this tip:

Tip 3: If your dog jumps up, look away, don't say anything and don't touch her. Then as soon as those four paws are all on the ground, bend down to her level and praise her lavishly, giving her as much fuss as you want.

Fuss her under her chin and on her chest - hands going over a dog's head can be scary and will encourage jumping up.

You also need to think about WHERE you greet your dog.

If you always greet your dog by your front door (or any door visitors usually arrive at) and you allow her to give you an exuberant, jumping up greeting, then you're encouraging your dog to be thinking about exuberant, jumping up greetings at that door. Don't be surprised if she then jumps up at your visitors.

Tip 4: Instead of having a cuddle session by the door as you come in from work, first put your coat away, or go into the kitchen and put the kettle on. Only then call your dog to you for as much fuss as you want - away from the door.

Dealing with visitors

Teaching dogs to greet people nicely is important. No-one likes getting jumped on, and the bigger the dog the more important it is. You're also at risk of being reported or sued if your dog frightens someone or injures them. Worse, your dog could end up being destroyed because of it. Tough but true.

Visitors are so exciting that your dog may find it really hard to control her exuberance, meaning she's highly likely to jump up. There are a number of options to prevent it. The key is to be prepared.

By the way, if you have more than one dog, it's best to avoid allowing them all to greet visitors at the door. Even if the dogs show acceptable greeting behaviour individually, when they convene at the door together they may excite one another too much while competing for the visitor's attention and your visitor will end up being jumped on.

It may sound obvious, but don't open the door until things are under control. Use any or all of the following options to help.

Tip 5: Putting your dog on a lead is simple, quick and easy. If your dog looks like he wants to jump at the visitor, then you can simply step back to prevent it.

Tip 6: Shut your dog away in another room while you deal with your visitor. This is often the best option when your visitor is not coming into the house or staying for long, for example, a delivery man, or meter reader, or a neighbour just wanting a quick chat.

Tip 7: Teach your dog to go to her bed or lie down on a mat. Just make sure she finds all sorts of tasty treats there to reward this great behaviour. This tip works best for visitors that are expected. Or have the bed or mat by the door, so you can reward your dog as the visitor enters.

If your visitor is coming into your house, use either tip

5 or 6 to help you manage the situation. It's often best to shut your dog away in another room while you bring your visitor in, get them settled and sort out refreshments. Then you can bring your dog in (on lead if necessary) to meet them.

Many people teach their dog to 'sit' to greet and this is a perfectly acceptable option, if it works. However, dogs can easily launch upwards from a sit and will then jump up into the visitor's face just as the visitor bends down to greet them. This can cause a nasty bruised nose. I generally prefer to have the dog standing to keep four paws on the ground, as it's more difficult for the dog to jump up from that position, but it's your choice.

How your visitor interacts with your dog is also important.

Tip 8: Ask your visitors to approach your dog with their hands held low, ready to tickle her under her chin, or rub her chest. ("She loves being tickled under her chin"). Approaching with hands down low and under your dog's head helps stop her wanting to jump up.

Tell visitors they should only interact with your dog when she is calm and has four paws on the floor. For friendly dogs, you can encourage the visitor to drop a treat on the floor for the dog as long as she has four paws on the ground. The dog can be sitting, lying down or standing, it doesn't really matter. But all four paws must be on the ground for her to get that treat.

Practice - then more practice - is the key to getting good results.

Tip 9: Use family or other regular visitors to help train your dog that four paws on the ground is a rewarding thing to do. Have a small pot of treats ready by the door and prime your visitors and all your family to pick some up as they come in. Humans should bend over or crouch down to greet your dog, while dropping treats one after the other, every half second or so, on the floor in front of the dog as they greet, pet and fuss her.

Meeting people out and about

Some dogs and some breeds attract strangers. Walking down the road with a fluffy cockapoo puppy will invite plenty of attention, whereas striding onwards with a large, adult German Shepherd or Doberman will tend to have the opposite effect.

I'm always amazed that complete strangers will approach an unknown owner and dog and ask to pet it (the dog, of course, not the owner: at least not in the circles I frequent). But then we're programmed to melt at the sight of a puppy with those gorgeous big eyes, cute face and silky coat.

Such encounters must be managed carefully so that you don't inadvertently allow your dog to learn to jump up or be rewarded for jumping up. I'm sure you've had the same interaction as I have - where the stranger says "It's OK, I don't mind dogs jumping up. Dogs love me." Well, I do mind my dog jumping up. I don't want him to be encouraged to jump up. On anyone, anywhere.

BHW: Only ever allow strangers to meet and pet your dog if you are sure your dog is comfortable with it and enjoys meeting new people. Watch him for any signs he's not comfortable and just walk away if he doesn't want any contact. It's OK to be rude to save your dog from unwanted attention.

If you want to allow the meeting, ask the stranger to greet your dog in a calm way by taking a sideways stance instead of looking at her head-on. Dogs generally perceive this as less threatening.

If you're happy to allow a greeting, suggest the person bends down (still staying sideways on) and tickles the dog under her chin or rubs her chest – this low approach is more polite and acceptable to dogs than allowing people to put their hands over the dog's head to pat her – which most dogs dislike anyway and that encourages them to jump up.

Allow the person to pet your dog gently for 3 seconds (or even just 2 seconds if you know your dog may jump up), then ask them to stand up and turn away. Move yourself and your dog away slightly, too, and praise and reward your dog for her great restraint in not jumping up. If you want to allow it, and your dog wants more fuss, she'll ask for it by moving back towards the person and/or leaning into them. But many dogs don't want prolonged attention from strangers, so this 'three second rule' is important.

Summary

- Make sure you (or any other family member or friend) are not inadvertently rewarding or teaching your dog to jump up
- Get down to your dog's level to fuss and pet them and to give and receive kisses
- Teach your dog that four paws on the floor is what gets and keeps human attention

There's one more reason that dogs might put their paws up on humans and that's what we'll look at in the next chapter – humping hounds.

5

HOW CAN I STOP MY DOG HUMPING?

Fred had come round to visit Colin and his dog, Spot. Colin and Fred were putting the world to rights over a cup of coffee, when Spot decided to indulge in one of his favourite pastimes of mounting and humping his bed. As Spot worked away, he and the bed moved closer to Fred. Colin decided to intervene. "Spot, stop that" he ordered. To his surprise, Spot stopped. The bed suddenly lost its allure and Spot fixed on Fred's leg as his next target. As Fred tried to push a determined Spot away, he raged at Colin, "Your dog is sex mad," he said, "You need to control him and stop him being so dominant." Colin tried not to laugh as he pulled Spot away. He muttered some sort of commitment to train Spot better.

Why do dogs hump?

Oh the embarrassment when your dog fastens onto your mum's leg with the grip of death and proceeds to rub unmentionable parts of his anatomy against her new cream linen trousers.

Or when your new boss has come for dinner and your dog drags his favourite cushion into the middle of the floor and proceeds to thrust away with abandon. A real conversation stopper, that one.

You may have been told that mounting and humping behaviour are a form of dominance, but, as you know from reading a previous chapter, this is not the case. Mounting and humping are normal dog behaviours.

Most puppies will show some humping behaviour, usually of soft items such as their bedding, teddy toy, or your Laura Ashley cushions. It's simply a way for them to play. Play is your dog's way of rehearsing the behaviours and skills which are important to the survival of himself and his species. It helps dogs rehearse reproduction behaviours.

Some dogs probably do it because, well, it feels good - it's the doggy method of masturbation.

There's a hormonal role in these behaviours, too. Adolescent dogs in the grip of humungous hormonal changes and surges may show more humping and mounting. Intact males and intact, 'in-heat' females often display inappropriate mounting - nearly always to prim Aunt Agatha or a dog-disliking friend, of course. Mounting behaviour may be seen for several months after neutering surgery in both dogs and bitches, until the sex hormones drop to their future low levels.

As with many behaviours, there can be medical reasons for your dog humping. If you notice the behaviour getting worse, or see your dog licking, biting or chewing excessively at his or her genitals, please take your dog to the vet for a check-up.

Medical causes of humping include urinary tract infections, urinary incontinence, vaginal infections, or skin allergies or anything else that causes itching, such as fleas. Rare causes can include retained ovaries after spaying and some tumours. It can cause some medical problems too, including paraphimosis, the posh name for when the penis gets 'stuck' and can't be retracted into the sheath, though this is unusual.

But by far the most common reasons for inappropriate humping are behavioural.

Some dogs, both neutered and intact, will perform this embarrassing social faux-'paw' to other dogs because they're socially inept and they see it as a form of social interaction or greeting. It's certainly not that they're trying to dominate the other dog and it usually isn't for amorous reasons. Although an entire male dog mounting an intact bitch in heat is definitely aimed at promulgation of the species.

Mounting other dogs can also be a (rather inappropriate) play behaviour. The best way to tell is by watching the other dog's reaction. If both dogs take turns and the mounting seems quite half-hearted then it's probably consensual play, but if your dog is humping away with a faraway gaze and the other dog is squirming underneath then it is not 'just play' and you'll need to intervene.

BHW: There's a risk your dog may get bitten by other dogs if he persists in trying to mount them, so always try to prevent the behaviour.

Mounting and humping of you, your family or your visitors can be your dog's way of getting attention. Dogs who hump people, or household items, often do it because it gets them attention from their owner. Remember, any attention, even if you're telling your dog off, is seen as good from the dog's point of view.

One of my previous dogs humped rarely, but he did it deliberately whenever we had visitors who weren't fond of dogs or who were the prim and proper type - he always knew. Once we'd settled down with drinks, Ben dragged a cushion into the middle of the room and proceed to hump away, right in front of the non-doggy visitor. I tried various things - ignoring it (difficult), laughing at it (the visitor never joined in) and trying to distract the visitor. That never worked either and the visitor got more and more sour-grape-faced as Ben focused on his actions right in front of her. When the visitor went I swear that dog was sniggering like Mutley about his activities. Mind you, so was I.

But most commonly, humping is a manifestation of stress, anxiety or insecurity in your dog. Perhaps something has changed - you moved house, or you got a new puppy, or a new baby, or you're just stressed about your job and your dog is picking up on it.

Perhaps he's anxious because you tell him off so much when he doesn't behave as you want. Or perhaps your dog is stressed because he's confused about what he can and can't do - can he lie on the sofa or not? Can he go upstairs or not? Are your house rules clear and is everyone in the family following them?

You can make humping worse by telling your dog off - because it'll make your dog more stressed and it'll increase the behaviour, not stop it. Try to work out what things might be stressing your dog and address those rather than the humping itself.

Humping can also occur when your dog becomes over-aroused or overstimulated. Perhaps you're having a party and there's lots of new people to meet. Or perhaps he gets over-excited when going out for a walk then tries to hump every passing dog he sees. Or perhaps he gets overstimulated by too much, or too prolonged, toy play.

When your dog is hyper he can't make sensible social decisions and his heightened excitement may be expressed as humping.

BHW: Be careful if you try to physically move your dog away from his humping focus as you may get bitten, especially if your dog is highly aroused or overstimulated.

So what can you do about it?

Working out *why* your dog is humping is the first step.

1) Have you excluded a medical reason? Check with your vet if you're unsure.

2) Does it seem to be hormonal? If the humping has recently started or got much worse in your 7 month- old dog, or if it only occurs when your bitch is in season, it's most likely to be hormone related. You could think about

neutering, or just wait it out for adolescent dogs, as it will probably settle down as the dog matures.

3) Is your dog seeking your attention? Difficult one to be sure of, this. Try noting when he humps and where. If it's always when you are with him but doing something else, and he stops if you yell at him, then it could be that he's doing it for attention.

4) Is it due to stress or anxiety? Stressed dogs may hump at any time, but if the humping is usually linked to a stressful event such as those mentioned above, or ongoing events, such as the children screaming and running around, or you've had visitors your dog doesn't know well, or after a walk where your dog's been barked at or jumped on by a strange dog, then stress is probably the cause. It's more difficult to tell if your dog humps because he finds life generally stressful, but his other behaviour may give you a hint - if he finds it difficult to relax, or if he's constantly on alert, for example, he may be chronically stressed.

5) Review your own behaviour, too. If you're constantly telling your dog off for his various misdemeanours you may be causing him stress, which may increase his humping.

6) Does it happen when your dog is over-excited? This one is generally easy to spot - your dog only humps when he goes into full-on excitement mode. There'll be other signs too, such as your dog doing the wall of death around your house, or jumping up like a pogo stick, or spinning in circles.

Once you've identified a possible reason for your dog

humping, you need to decide if you want to stop it. Humping isn't dangerous to your dog and he probably enjoys it, otherwise he wouldn't do it. But if it worries or embarrasses you and you want to do something about it, here are a few things that can help:

Tip 1: Neutering may be the best first option. It can reduce humping behaviour, if you think your dog is humping for sexual or hormonal reasons.

Tip 2: For some dogs, simply removing the object they prefer to hump (a special cushion, toy, or particular bedding) may reduce or stop the behaviour.

Tip 3: Do some training to teach him an alternative behaviour instead - 'settle' or 'stay' are good options. Teach him to 'leave it', or teach 'off' to interrupt the behaviour - just make sure he gets a brilliant, yummy reward for doing so. See my book, *Pesky Puppy to Perfect Pet*, if you want to know how to teach these to your dog. Or find a good local training class.

Tip 4: If you can spot when your dog is most likely to perform the behaviour, have a plan to distract him with something else instead, such as a filled Kong or food puzzle toy such as a Kong Wobbler, or a snuffle mat. There are lots of good food toys on the market nowadays.

If your dog is easily over-aroused, or you think your dog does it because he's stressed, you need to help him relax by finding other outlets for him. Try giving him more exercise, especially exercise that makes him work his brain. Let him use his nose to sniff whatever he wants instead of power walking with him. Playing scent games such as finding hidden toys or food is always satisfyingly tiring for dogs.

Tip 5: Make sure you always keep your dog on lead when near other dogs if you know he has a humping tendency and might decide the other dog is a good target.

Tip 6: If you think your dog is using the behaviour to seek attention from you ("Look, dad, I'm doing that thing you don't like again") then get up and leave the room when he starts - if you are not there he can't get the reward he wants. As soon as he stops (watch through the door jamb or use clever technology like a webcam - just don't ask me how to work it), go back in and praise him well for not humping. Perhaps play with him with a tug toy, or do some training. And think about how you can give him more attention without him needing to hump to get it.

Finally, always seek professional help if you're worried, if the behaviour is excessively frequent or if your dog does it only at certain times or in certain situations.

Humping is a normal behaviour which your dog probably enjoys. A lot of the time you probably don't need to do anything about it and many dogs don't hump as much as they get older, anyway. However, if your dog is humping because he's stressed then it will improve his quality of life significantly if you can reduce or remove the cause of his stress - which will then reduce the humping.

Summary

- Work out why your dog might be mounting and humping
- Neutering helps for hormonal related humping
- Other reasons need other solutions
- Stress is a common reason for humping

Talking of stress, in the next chapter we're going to talk about something that stresses many owners – if their dog licks them too much.

6

HOW DO I STOP MY DOG LICKING SO MUCH?

Barbara felt sick. How could Kathryn allow her dog to do that? As they were sitting having a cup of tea and a traybake, Barbara had been watching Rover thoroughly wash his private parts. Rover then went up to Kathryn, jumped up at her and gave her face a good licking. Barbara struggled not to let her disgust show. She didn't mind dogs licking her hands - after all, they were easy to wash - but her face was definitely off limits, especially when she knew where that prehensile, drooly tongue had just been.

Why does your dog lick?

Who doesn't secretly love those doggy welcome kisses?

Your dog is showing how much he loves you, isn't he?

Of course, he licks other things besides you. Different areas of his body (including some unmentionable bits), his food bowl, your sticky hands after eating that doughnut, his doggy friends - licking is such a common behaviour.

But *why* do dogs lick?

As always - it depends. There are many reasons.

Licking starts in the litter. Puppies instinctively lick their mother's mouth because in the wild, that causes her to regurgitate the food she has been out to find for them - eating it herself is the easiest way to carry it home.

Dogs enjoy licking us as a show of affection. Some dogs lick much more than others, it's an individual thing. Licking for affection releases endorphins in the dog - and in us. Endorphins are feel-good hormones, so it's a pleasurable activity for both human and dog.

Some dogs just love the salty taste of our skin, or may particularly like the taste of our soap or body wash.

Dogs often lick us more when we return home, because licking picks up scent molecules that tell the dog where we've been and who we've been consorting with.

Perhaps it's a good thing dogs can't talk... Gus always has a good sniff and sometimes a lick at me when I've been out with clients or friends. Daughter no. 1 coined this behaviour with the descriptive phrase "the scent of betrayal".

Dogs will often lick objects as a form of exploration. Your dog's tongue contains lots of sensory cells which helps them find out about what things are and what they're made of. If they find they like the sensation, they may continue to lick that particular object - similar to a child who finds it soothing to suck a blanket corner. The favourite lick object may be a particular curtain or cushion, or their bedding, a particular toy, or a household object such as a door stop, towel, cupboard door - more or less anything, actually.

Licking unusual things such as walls or floors, or if your dog is licking her lips frequently, can be a sign of nausea or gastrointestinal upset. One study from Canada showed that 74% of dogs who showed this behaviour had some sort of gastrointestinal problem - and once that was treated the licking reduced or stopped.

Some dogs may lick to get attention - it can be difficult to ignore a determined licker, so they usually get exactly what they want. They might also lick because they're hungry, or bored, or just want some fuss and attention, which was the case with Rover.

Stress can be a cause of licking. Licking is calming to dogs - just as thumb sucking can be to humans, because it releases those lovely, relaxing endorphins. The stress may be external, such as loud noises, or other changes in the environment, or it may have an internal cause such as separation from you when you go out to work.

Dogs who lick from chronic stress can often lick all the fur off certain areas of their body, which can lead to skin infections and painful lumps called 'acral lick granulomas' (I've told you before how much we behaviourists love grand-sounding words.)

Excessive licking may be due to allergy. Allergic dogs may lick obsessively between their toes, enough to stain the fur, or they may lick or chew at their inner thighs or hind legs. Environmental allergies are caused by dusts, pollens, and other airborne particles which can build up on the skin and fur of your dog and in turn cause itching. Allergies to flea bites can cause similar signs.

BHW: *There are also some obsessive-compulsive licking disorders, some of which are breed specific. These can be damaging to your dog's health, so if you suspect this is the case with your pooch, seek professional help.*

I had one case recently where the gorgeous, friendly dog licked their humans and the home environment excessively, obsessively and continually. She ended up with a huge furball, which required surgery - and the owners ended up with a huge vet bill. I'll be telling her story in more detail in a future book in this series.

Finally, there are a range of other medical problems that might cause excessive licking. These include:

- a foreign body or object, especially in a paw or mouth

- anal gland irritation - licking their bottom - perhaps not a good idea to have a kissy session with your pooch after this...

- dental disease or oral problems

- hunger or dehydration

- nausea

- dementia

- neurological problems - canine distemper has more or less vanished, but it can cause a behaviour called "chewing gum fits," a specific form of licking.

Spend some time watching your dog to find out what the most likely cause of their licking might be.

What can you do about licking?

You may want to do nothing. Even if your friends stop visiting.

If you look forward to cuddles and kisses with your pooch, and you both enjoy it, feel free to carry on and relish that lovely rush of endorphins.

Tip 1: If you don't want a daily face-wash, you could encourage your dog to lick other areas of your body instead, such as your hands, which are more easily washed.

Many dogs use licking, sometimes alongside other behaviours such as jumping up or pawing, to get your attention. It's really difficult to ignore a doggy face pressed close to yours, or a moist tongue splashed across your chops.

Rover uses all three of these behaviours to get Kathryn's attention - and it works. It's quite disconcerting trying to have a conversation with Kathryn when there are so many interruptions from Rover demanding attention.

And once he's satisfied with the attention he has from Kathryn, he'll transfer that attention to anyone else in the room. He'll come and sit beside you, pushing into your legs and licking at your hands. If that fails, or you pull your hands away, he'll jump up.

If your dog licks you to get attention, first you need to realise that's what's happening. Then you can decide on how best to respond.

Tip 2: You could ignore the behaviour until it stops -

although many dogs can be really persistent with this, especially if it's worked well in the past.

Tip 3: You could offer a food or chew toy for them to work out their licking needs on. Licki mats are flat or shaped plastic textured mats that can sit on the floor or be fixed to a wall. Smear something over it - wet dog food, cheese spread, meat paste - whatever your dog loves, and your dog will spend some time happily licking the food off it instead of covering you with slobbery kisses. There's a huge variety of lick mats and snuffle mats available out there - have a browse round for something that will suit your dog.

Tip 4: Teach your dog some decent basic behaviours such as sit, down, or wait/stay so you can tell your dog to do something more acceptable instead of jumping all over you and licking you. Teaching your dog to hold a toy in his mouth will also stop him from licking you.

Your dog may just love what's on your skin. The signs of that are prolonged and persistent licking at any bare skin - it can give you a queer shock if you bend down and expose some fresh skin...

Tip 5: If you find a near total body wash annoying, you can try changing your body wash, soap or perfume - though your dog may like the new one even more, of course.

But if you're worried that your dog's licking may be a sign of something else going on, or some form of distress, you may want to change or do something to help.

For bored dogs, giving them more to do is the key.

Tip 6: Keeping your dog's mind and body occupied

with more exercise and training. Chew and food toys can help if boredom is contributing to excessive licking.

Perhaps you've noticed that your dog's licking is seasonal. In spring or summer that might indicate an allergic cause, but in winter there are some direct causes of irritation, especially to the feet and legs, which can cause your dog to lick a lot - road salt is one such suspect in winter and sea salt is a problem in summer.

Tip 7: Checking and washing your dog's paws after coming in from walks in winter, can help reduce licking due to irritation from impacted snow or road salt, and in summer from grass seeds caught in the toes or salt from the sea.

BHW: If your dog loves to paddle or swim in the sea, always wash them down afterwards as otherwise they will be tempted to lick the salt from their fur and feet as it dries, which is dangerous for their health.

Tip 8: Prevent flea infestations by giving your dog appropriate flea (and worm) prevention. Newer flea treatments come in pleasant tablet form which most dogs will scoff quite happily - no more trying to keep your dog still while you drop cold liquid onto a patch of skin between their shoulders.

If you suspect your dog is stressed - perhaps he only licks in certain circumstances, or looks worried while he works that tongue - try to identify what the cause of the stress might be then find ways to address it.

Ask for professional behavioural help if you need. And there's much more about stress in book 2 in this series...

If you think your dog might be allergic to something, or

if you suspect there might be a medical cause, take your dog to your vet for a full check-up.

Your vet will also advise on drugs to help obsessive-compulsive licking alongside a behaviour modification programme (that's my job) - more on this in a later book.

Kathryn is a single lady whose main relationship is with her dog. Both she and Rover were quite happy with the status quo and she saw no reason to change anything.

I don't know if Barbara kept visiting or not.

Summary

- Licking is a normal dog behaviour which is calming for both your dog and you
- There are many causes of excessive licking, so some detective work may be required
- Seek vet help if you're concerned about a medical cause
- Seek behavioural help if you suspect an underlying behavioural problem

Having discussed one disagreeable problem, we'll discuss in the next chapter what to do about the obnoxious fluid and solid messes that your dog might produce in your home.

7

HOW CAN I STOP MY DOG PEEING AND POOING IN THE HOUSE?

A nna desperately needed help. She'd already replaced her rug once and knew the carpet had to be next, but she didn't want to waste her hard-earned cash buying something that would be ruined again soon. Sooty was a lovely dog in so many ways but at 6 months old Anna felt he really should be house-trained by now. His favourite wee spot was the rug in front of the fireplace and his favourite poo spot was behind the settee. She'd followed the advice she was given about taking him out regularly, but it didn't seem to make any difference. Anna's neighbour, Fred, who's always had dogs, suggested Anna should "rub his nose in it" to stop him doing it.

Maggie had an unusual problem. She loved her two 10 month-old Labrador brothers dearly and they seemed to love each other too. Except that most days, as they were mooching round the house, Bonzo cocked his leg on Beano, peeing on his head or legs - it didn't seem to matter where. How on earth could she stop this unpleasant habit?

Why do dogs eliminate in the home?

Peeing and pooing in the house is one of the most "eww"-worthy bad behaviours. Eliminating in the home is unpleasant for everyone, especially the person who has to clear it up. Usually the female...

Puppies, like babies, just wee and poo when they need to - wherever they are. You need to teach your puppy where to 'go'. It's difficult to avoid accidents with a young puppy in the first few weeks, but once the puppy understands where it should eliminate, house soiling will cease.

Most puppies can be clean and dry in the house by around 4 months old, if you've been obsessive about taking them out regularly and properly cheered all their outside performances.

Puppies are not physiologically mature enough to hold everything in at night until they're around 13-14 weeks old. You can create a toileting area in their bed area or crate until then, with a puppy pad (one of the few good uses for the horrid things), or newspaper. Alternatively, set your alarm and get up to take the puppy out at say 3am, then each night set the alarm 10-15 minutes later until the pup is sleeping through the night and stays clean and dry.

So why do some dogs seem to find it so difficult to learn not to pee and poo in the house?

If your pooch has an accident in the home, especially if it always happens in the same place, the most common reason is because a trace of scent remains from a previous pee or poo. If you don't clean accidents properly, your puppy will be attracted back to the same place to eliminate there again - and again.

Needless to say, Fred's advice is useless. Rubbing your dog's nose in any mess he's made is pointless. He's completely forgotten he made the mess, so all you're doing is something that's unpleasant for your puppy and might make him scared of you.

The second big reason pups learn to toilet inside your home is that you've used....I'm struggling to say the words....I hate them so much....*puppy pads*. These things are impregnated with scent to attract your pup to pee and poo there. But where do you put them? *Inside the house.* So what are you teaching your pup to do? Pee and poo *inside the house.*

BHW: *Don't use puppy pads.*

There are several other reasons for soiling in the home.

Some dogs can leak urine when they become aroused or excited. It's an involuntary thing. It can be related to being in a particular location or with particular people, most often when visitors arrive or first thing in the morning when you greet your puppy.

Lack of training is another reason. Dogs don't generalise training easily, so just because they understand they shouldn't pee and poo in your house, doesn't mean they understand not to do it in other people's houses. It's always worth taking your pooch outside to eliminate when going anywhere new so you can reinforce this.

Some dogs may inadvertently learn to eliminate inside at a particular spot. This usually happens when you've missed the signs your pup needed to eliminate, so they found a handy spot to perform and you missed the whole thing. Such favourite toilet spots are usually behind a sofa (like with Sooty) or door, where they're easily missed.

Dogs prefer certain types of surface to perform their eliminations (which is why your favourite rug is always at risk with a new puppy), so if the floor surfaces in another house are different to yours, your pooch may express his joy at finding a favourite type of surface he doesn't have in his own house and eliminate there.

Or perhaps you're struggling to train him to eliminate outside in your paved yard - many pups dislike peeing on concrete (so would I. Think about the splashing...)

Inappropriate house soiling can also be due to a number of medical problems, so always get your pet checked out by your vet, especially if the problem occurs after your dog has been clean and dry for a time.

Digestion problems, inflammatory problems, or neurological problems can all cause inappropriate soiling.

Medical reasons for inappropriate peeing include renal problems, infections and physical changes. And, unfortunately, the ageing processes can also result in dogs starting to pee and poo in the house.

Why do dogs mark things with pee?

Dogs pee on things principally to mark territory and leave pee-mails for canine friends. It's generally acceptable outdoors, but not inside a house.

Dogs use urine to leave a scent signal to say "I'm here". All owners of male dogs understand their dog's need to stop at every lamppost and bush, have a good sniff to 'read' the pee-mail, then cock their leg to over-mark any existing scent with their own message.

To mark, a dog will lift their leg up high and twist the rest of their body, which means they can spray their mark as high as possible. Height means status in the doggy world. The higher the squirt, the more the scent is spread around the area by the wind, too.

Cocking a leg also means the dog can be more accurate about hitting the mark, as it were - although anyone who has watched Gus will see that most of the time his aim is well off. Our bathroom floor sometimes shows that Himself's aim can be off at times, too. It seems to be a common male trait.

Cocking a leg to mark is also seen in foxes and wolves. Cats, too, use urine to mark, but they don't lift their leg. Rather, tomcats will back up to their target and then squirt from their rear.

Bitches will mark using a "squat raise", though they rarely mark as much as male dogs. Neutered dogs still mark frequently, though entire males generally mark the most. The deposited scent can also communicate reproductive status - bitches often only mark, or mark more, when they're in heat.

Marking is also used to indicate possession. That's why some dogs will pee on their owner's beds, or on certain toys. That spray of urine contains pheromones which leave a message in neon lights that says to other dogs, "This is mine". Urine when marking, unlike when just peeing, is mixed with a fatty substance which make the scent hang around longer.

Marking inside the home is an unpleasant problem. It often occurs when there's another dog, or dogs, in the same household, or, rarely, frequent visiting dogs. It's most common when there are persistent, regular spats between two (or more) dogs in the same house. Such fights may be about perceived status, or attention from their humans, or access to a particular area or place.

BHW: *This scenario needs behaviourist help. Get in touch.*

Marking inside can also result from anxiety and frustration, or if your dog feels threatened. Perhaps a new dog has moved in nearby, or there are unusual noises, or scary storms, or the dog is excited by a postman arriving, or there's been the arrival of a new family member, human or canine.

The raging hormones of adolescence can cause a flood of marking (see what I did there?) as the dog flexes his testosterone driven muscles.

If you have an older dog who suddenly starts marking inappropriately, get a vet check - there may be an underlying medical condition causing the problem. Or it may be because of some change in the household or routine.

So there could be a number of reasons why Maggie's dog Bonzo pees on his sibling, Beano.

When do dogs start to mark?

The main trigger for marking is the testosterone surge that occurs at puberty, anytime from five to twelve months of age or so, depending on your dog's breed. For most dogs, puberty is around six to nine months and most dogs will start cocking their leg around then.

But some dogs mature much later than others, so may not start cocking their leg until they're well over a year old, even up to two years of age.

Cocking a leg is also a learned behaviour. Male dogs will copy other male dogs and learn to cock their legs and mark. How often have you seen a dog watch another dog sniff and mark then go over to that place and do exactly the same?

Dogs who've been neutered early, before their puberty hormone surge, sometimes never mark, but many early-neutered dogs will start to mark at some point, just from copying other male dogs.

Dogs that aren't territorial may never bother marking and dogs who live with all female dogs may also never mark, because there's no role model.

What can you do about unwanted elimination or marking?

There's one key message - make sure you concentrate on teaching your puppy or new dog where it's acceptable for him to pee and poo. You can housetrain a dog at any age, but it's easiest when they're puppies. It's the same process - take them out regularly, and after eating, playing and sleeping, then praise the heck out of them when they perform.

Yes, it takes time and yes, it's vital to watch your pup

or new dog like a hawk for the first few weeks, but it's so important to get this stage right. Get hold of a copy of my book, *Pesky Puppy to Perfect Pet*, available from Amazon, for more information, or download the free advice sheet from our website.

So what can you do if your dog produces unwanted pees or poos in your home?

Tip 1: If you catch your dog peeing or urine marking (or even preparing to pee or mark) a surface inside the house, quickly interrupt him with a sharp noise, such as "oops" or "eeek", and take him outside. Then reward and praise him for choosing to urinate outdoors.

Leaking urine when excited is most common in bitches. Nearly all of them will grow out of this unpleasant habit after a few months, but it's a subconscious reaction and not under any conscious control, so you can't tell your dog off or get cross - it's not her fault, she can't help it.

Tip 2: Try to manage excitement peeing by keeping all meetings and greetings as calm as possible to reduce the risk of it happening.

Tip 3: If there is any elimination accident, it's essential to make sure you've removed any lingering scent from soiled areas. Don't use household cleaners because most of these add scent to an area rather than remove it. Use a pet odour neutraliser to thoroughly clean any soiled area of remaining scent.

You can also clean the area with a steam cleaner then liberally use pet deodoriser. If you haven't got, or can't get, a good pet deodoriser, use a mix of one part biological washing powder to ten parts water.

If you're concerned there might be a medical problem behind the peeing and pooing, please take your pup to the vet for a thorough check up.

Tip 4: Neutering can reduce, though not eliminate, marking in males and females and is the option of choice when the cause of bothersome marking is most probably raging hormones.

BHW: Don't let adolescent marking in the home become a habit - deal with it as soon as you can by asking for expert behaviourist help.

Tip 5: Deal with anything that might be causing anxiety or frustration in your dog. Perhaps you need to limit your dog's access to the front windows, or bedrooms, or stop your other dog or children pestering him.

Tip 6: Ask for help from a qualified behaviourist (me) if you're worried the cause of marking might be conflict between your dogs or if your dog is marking different objects and areas excessively around the home.

Finally, of course, make sure you're giving your dog enough outside exercise so he has plenty of time and opportunity to pee and poo appropriately. Always pick up your dog's poo of course, every time. No excuses.

Sooty preferred to pee on Anna's nice, soft rug instead of their small, fully paved yard area. His pooing behind the sofa was from habit because Anna hadn't made sure she'd cleaned the scent from the area.

We decided to re-train Sooty to use a large tray filled with grass and gravel outside. Anna followed my advice and persevered with great success. At my final visit she proudly showed off her pristine new carpet and rug.

Bonzo's marking of Beano was related to surging adolescent hormones. Neutering both dogs, then a few weeks of making sure they were otherwise entertained in separate areas of the house, had plenty of walks and training to make them physically and mentally tired, and teaching them behaviours such as lie down and settle, solved the problem.

Summary

- Peeing and pooing in the home may result from insufficient or inadequate housetraining or because there is some remaining scent attracting dogs to eliminate at favourite spots
- Marking in the home may result from some form of conflict, anxiety or frustration and will often need dog behaviourist help
- Neutering can reduce, though not always eliminate, marking

Pee and poo aren't the only things that can destroy your fixtures and fittings. Read on and we'll discuss the frustrating problem of the destroyer dog...

8

HOW DO I STOP MY DOG DESTROYING THINGS?

Margaret despaired. She never realised getting a dog would be so difficult. She looked ruefully at her dining table chairs. Their legs were pitted and scratched from Poppy's chewing. At least most of the chair chewing had stopped now Poppy was nearly a year old. But Poppy still chewed things when Margaret went out. It was always Margaret's things - shoes, bras, slippers. Anything soft and smelling of Margaret seemed to be fair game. "Why mine and not my husband's?" Margaret moaned to Fred. "Do I have to put up with this?" "You need to show her who's boss," said Fred, "Tell her off and smack her when she's naughty." Margaret was unhappy at this advice so she sensibly sought my professional help.

Why do dogs chew?

Chewing is a natural behaviour for your dog, because he explores this crazy, busy, colourful world he's entered with his mouth. It's how he learns about textures, scents and tastes; how he works out what things are, what sorts of things are pleasant to chew and which aren't. After all, dogs don't have hands with opposable digits like we do.

As your pup grows and starts teething, he *needs* to chew to help set his adult teeth into his jaw. Chewing helps to relieve the pain and discomfort from teething. (Think about how our human babies like to mouth things while they're teething, too.)

The big chewing stage is between 16 and 22 weeks of age, the main teething phase. But there's a second chewing stage, sometimes called the exploratory stage. This happens in adolescent dogs usually between around six and ten months of age. Just when you think your favourite chairs and table are safe, those sharp, now adult, teeth start another attack. Adolescent dogs seem to get an insatiable urge to chew - possibly from gum discomfort as their adult teeth are settling into their jaws.

Chewing is nature's way of keeping your dog's jaws strong and their teeth clean. (Humans chew gum for much the same reasons.) Chewing bones and other hard objects helps keep your dog's teeth healthy and reduce tartar and plaque. Encouraging your dog to chew appropriate things is good for them and for your monetary health too - dental problems are the main cause of vet bills in young adult dogs.

BHW: Never leave your dog alone with any sort of hard chew that could splinter. Dogs can easily choke on bits that break off chews or plastic toys.

The other main reason for chewing is emotional.

- Chewing is an outlet for frustration.

If your dog can see people, other dogs, birds or animals close or passing by but can't get to them to meet, or chase, them, the frustration that results can make her bite, shake and destroy the nearest object, such as your best cushions. (You can see this on walks, too - frustration can cause biting and chewing at the lead. More about this in book 2 of this series.)

- Chewing can relieve boredom.

Some dogs simply don't get enough mental or physical exercise. Bored dogs look for other ways to entertain themselves and many turn to chewing and destruction. Dogs need both mind and body exercise. Happily tired dogs tend not to chew inappropriately.

- Chewing can relieve stress.

Being crated can be stressful if not introduced well or boring if your dog is left in her crate for too long.

Being close by another animal your dog doesn't get on well with, such as your cat or other dog, can be stressful.

Upsets such as moving home, changes in relationships such as divorce, new partners coming to live in the home, having children - all these are stressful for us and for our pets.

I used to suck my thumb as a child, then bite my nails as a teenager when I got anxious. (To my shame, I still chew my cuticles occasionally.) I also nibble at food when

I'm stressed or bored. There's something about using your mouth that's comforting - for us and our dogs.

Puppies (and older dogs) will search out things that smell strongly of "their" person, especially when the person is not there. The scent itself is comforting and the act of chewing is doubly comforting.

Why was Poppy stealing and chewing Margaret's things and not her husbands? Several reasons:

- Perhaps she identifies more strongly with Margaret than with her husband

- Margaret's things may just be more easily accessible to her

- She may simply prefer Margaret's scent to that of her husband

Don't punish chewing

I hope I don't have to tell you to ignore Fred's advice to tell your puppy off when she's chewing things, and of course, you should never smack her.

Punishment based methods don't stop behaviour - though they sometimes suppress it to some extent. But it's the longer term fall out that matters.

Telling your dog off has unwanted effects.

Your dog may stop trusting you.

She may become sneaky about her chewing, making sure she only does it when you're not around.

She may become frightened of you, or associate the telling off with a particular place or situation, which will result in her becoming scared of that place or situation in future, producing its own problems.

At worst, she may decide she needs to use aggression to stop you being aggressive to her.

BHW: Never tell your dog off and never, ever smack her for doing something you see as wrong but is natural for her

So what can you do about your dog's chewing?

Chewing is normal

Dogs can spend hours chewing away on bones, sticks or anything else that's available - including their bedding. It's important to provide lots of appropriate chew toys and teach your puppy what's OK to chew and what's not.

Most dogs like edible chews such as pigs ears and rawhide bones. Enthusiastic chewers may like stag bars or antlers, which are nice and hard to gnaw on. Other dogs may prefer to chew on softer toys, or plastic chew toys.

BHW: Vets may advise against antlers or other hard objects because of the risk of your dog breaking a tooth. Decide for yourself if your dog's enjoyment is worth the small risk of a tooth breaking. Talk with your vet about which chews are safe for your dog if you're unsure.

The wide variety of Kongs also provides a great chewing outlet for your dog.

Test things out with your own pooch.

Give her a variety of things to chew and see which become favourites. However, I'd advise against giving her old shoes or slippers - she'll get confused about which footwear can be chewed and which are out of bounds. You don't want to risk your new Guccis being shredded.

Whatever types of acceptable things you find your dog loves to chew, buy several and rotate them so she doesn't get bored with them.

If you give her an outlet for her chewing she'll leave your precious possessions in peace.

But my dog chews things to pieces

If your dog does something bad while you're out, there really is no point getting cross with her.

She'll never make the association between your displeasure and the dismembered settee, table, shoe or slipper. I know you think she knows "because she looks guilty", but believe me, she doesn't. What she *will* make an association with is you coming home and being cross - she hasn't a clue it was what she did that caused your anger.

That look does not signify guilt. She's actually showing you what we call appeasement gestures (we dog trainers do like big words to describe things) - that is, body postures and facial expressions that are designed to say "I'm just a worm, please don't be cross with me, I hate you being cross".

If the house is a bomb site when you come home, just clear it up and work out what you need to do to stop it happening again. Such as, do you need to engage a dog walker? Or ask your neighbour to pop in? Should you plan to give her a longer walk and some training before you go out?

There are a few behaviour problems that can result in destructive chewing. If you think your dog has any of these problems, you'll benefit from asking for behaviourist help.

- Dogs who chew only, or most intensely, when left alone, may be using chewing to relieve the stress of separation. They'll often show other signs too, such as whining, barking, pacing, restlessness and soiling the home.

- Some dogs become obsessed with licking, sucking and chewing fabrics. This can be due to being weaned too early (before 7-8 weeks). If your pooch is difficult to distract from this sort of behaviour and/or does it for lengthy periods of time, it may have become a compulsive behaviour and this needs urgent behaviourist help.

- Dogs on a diet may chew more, especially objects that are related to, or smell like, food.

What can I do to stop my dog chewing?

If your dog destroys her bedding, your knickers, shoes, slippers or household fixtures and fittings, the first thing to do is to work out why she might be doing it.

Puppies chew. They chew a lot at first. If you're struggling with your puppy's chewing, try the following tips:

Tip 1: To prevent your favourite Jimmy Choos, slippers, or undergarments being destroyed, make sure you keep all that seductive smelly stuff out of reach of your inquisitive, determined puppy.

Tip 2: When you catch your dog chewing inappropriate items, such as your shoes or slippers, redirect the chewing onto a more appropriate item, like a chew toy or stuffed Kong. Then praise your pup for selecting an acceptable outlet for her chewing behaviour.

Tip 3: Leave your puppy with appropriate chew toys when you go out, such as a filled Kong, favourite rubber bone or similar. Nothing that might break or splinter, obviously.

Tip 4: Use appropriate barriers (doors and baby gates) to stop her exploring where you'd rather she didn't.

Or perhaps your older dog chews inappropriate items in your home, especially hard furniture such as tables and chair legs. She may be telling you she needs suitable things to chew. In that case:

Tip 5: Make sure your dog has suitable hard chews. Dentastix, nylabones and antlers can all be favourites - just be aware of the risk of your dog breaking a tooth on hard objects. Vigilance is essential.

If you think there might be an emotional reason for her chewing, try to work out what that is.

Is it to relieve stress or boredom?

Or if it only happens when you go out and leave her, it may be a sign she's struggling to cope when being left alone.

Tip 6: Make sure your dog is well exercised in both mind and body before you leave her - a good walk incorporating some training is the easiest way to do this.

Tip 7: Look for any obvious causes of stress. Is she frustrated by not being able to get at the people, dogs, cats, birds, cars or vans that pass her wide-screen live TV window? If so, leave her where she can't see out - in a back room, utility room, kitchen or crate.

If she's stressed by another animal in your home, keep them separated when you go out.

If your dog struggles to cope when you go out then that's the main problem, not the chewing. I'll be dealing fully with separation anxiety in another book, as it's a big subject.

Anything more than being unhappy you're leaving, or chewing the odd sock, needs more specialist help. Make sure you follow the tips above and ask for help from your friendly KC accredited behaviourist (that's me, by the way), if following this advice doesn't help the problem.

Or perhaps you suspect your dog may have been taken from her litter too early because she's obsessed with chewing fabric items.

Tip 8: You may be able to help her by giving her old fabric pillowcases or blankets to chew while you're out, but if she chews obsessively please seek professional help. I'll be looking more closely at obsessive behaviours in a future book in this series.

Poppy's chewing was mainly related to boredom. She chewed Margaret's things rather than her husbands because Margaret's things tended to be left lying around and also because she had bonded more closely with Margaret than with her husband.

The first solution was for Margaret to keep her things tidied away. Giving Poppy more mental exercise and leaving suitable chew and food toys for her when Margaret went out solved the problem.

Summary

- Dogs are natural chewers and puppies chew more when they're teething
- Boredom, stress or frustration are common causes of excessive chewing and destruction
- Finding appropriate and satisfying chew items for your dog can help
- If the chewing is excessive or prolonged, please seek expert help

Some dogs love to attack and chew moving things – let's look at why your dog hates the hoover in the next chapter.

9

HELP! MY DOG ATTACKS THE HOOVER

The balls of dog hair were building up and rolling down the hall like tumbleweed. Sandra had put it off as long as possible, but she really was going to have to clean and hoover. Taking a deep breath, she went to the cupboard. As she opened it, Benji's face appeared round the doorway. She pulled the hoover out and Benji charged across the hall. She wrestled with the machine, while Benji barked and barked, charging at it, trying to chase this infernal contraption out of the house to be banished for ever. Turning it on made things even worse, turning Benji into a manic, growling, biting, whirling dervish. The hoover was scratched and pit-marked all over from his attention. Brushes and mops were as bad and Sandra had had to replace three already this year. She was desperate. She couldn't imagine how she would ever manage to clean her house properly again.

Why do dogs attack hoovers?

Trying to control your frantic, barking, lunging pooch while trying to clean your home is no fun.

And it's a common problem.

It's not too surprising if you think about it. Brushes and mops move back and forth along the floor, erratically, in just the right way to attract attention from your pooch and stimulate his prey drive. Some dogs are a bit frightened by brushes and mops, but many others see them as play objects and enjoy trying to leap on them, grab them and shake them ferociously in a great game.

The majority of dogs dislike vacuum cleaners. These brightly coloured, scary monsters tend to have odd shaped pieces attached, they blow out air and suck it in strongly and we humans appear to wrestle with them. They're noisy even to our ears and most produce a range of high frequency sounds which are anathema to sensitive doggy hearing. Worse still, if your dog runs away to hide under a table or chair, the vacuum cleaner follows and chases him.

There may also be a scent element to these behaviours. Moving the vacuum cleaner around stirs up clouds of dust and scent which may be overwhelming for our scent sensitive pets. And if your dog goes to sniff at it, it sniffs back even more powerfully.

No wonder many dogs are confused and aren't sure whether to approach it or avoid it. Gus chooses the latter option - he takes himself off into a different room when I vacuum and keeps well away.

BHW: *Some dogs may be truly terrified by these household*

*monsters - and can injure themselves trying to escape. Please
seek help if this describes your dog.*

That pesky prey drive all dogs have is easily stimulated
by household cleaning tools. Herding breeds may try and
herd brushes, mops and hoovers, and terrier breeds may
try to kill them. Both approaches work, as eventually the
hoover is turned off, the brushing and mopping stops and
the scary objects are put away.

The dog can then go and rest, satisfied that he has
saved the household from attack once again. Dogs will
never understand the hygienic purpose of such tools.

What can I do about it?

Good breeders introduce the sights, sounds and smells of
hoovers, brushes and mops as well as other household
appliances and noises from early on in the puppy's life.
Puppies brought up in this way enter their new homes
primed to cope with all the bustle, noise and movement of
cleaning tools.

Some dogs may have an innate fear of noisy, moving
things, so new owners may have to battle against this
primal self-preservation urge. In my experience, fear is
usually the underlying emotion in dogs who either run
away from or attack the hoover.

So what can you do about it?

There are two main approaches. Management may be
the best and easiest option, especially if your dog is one of
the few who sees attacking the hoover as a fun game.

Tip 1: Hoover, brush and mop only when your dog is

out for a walk with your partner, or put your dog out in the (safely enclosed) garden or a distant room with a long-lasting chew toy while you clean.

Tip 2: If you can, get a cleaner. You can leave her (or him) to it, take your dog out for a walk and come back to a lovely clean house.

I sometimes dream of going the whole hog and having a housekeeper. Imagine not having to think about what to eat day after day and leaving someone else to do all the cleaning and tidying. Well, we can all dream...

For the sake of your dog's mental health you may want to help your scared pooch learn to cope better with mops, brushes and hoovers.

It's a lengthy process, but it is possible to teach your dog to be relaxed about them. We behaviourists have some big words for this process - counterconditioning (teaching your dog to like something he was previously afraid of) and desensitisation (gradually increasing the intensity of the feared thing). There'll be more about this important concept in another book.

Be warned, it is a prolonged process and you can only progress at the speed your dog can cope with.

Each of the steps I outline below can take several days or even weeks. You need bucketloads of patience - and bucketloads of treats for your dog.

BHW: If you want to try this, please get help from a behaviourist to make the process as quick and easy as possible for your sake and for your dog's. It's not something to be taken on half-heartedly.

Here's a brief outline of how you do it.

Start with the hoover (or mop, or brush) just sitting there in plain view. If your dog reacts like Benji to the hoover coming out of the cupboard, you may need to start by just opening the cupboard door so he can see it.

Feed your dog some tasty treats on the opposite side of the room. As long as he stays relaxed, you can gradually get nearer and nearer the machine. Take it at your dog's pace of course, never try to rush things. You want your dog to be totally relaxed and happy being near the inert, unmoving hoover - your aim is for him to ignore it.

Once your dog can happily approach and be beside the non-moving, turned-off hoover with no problems, put some treats on it and let your dog eat them. You want to teach him the hoover is a nice thing, not a scary thing or a fun toy.

Then, keeping the hoover switched off, give your dog a juicy filled Kong on his bed or somewhere else safe and out of the way while you start to move the hoover (or mop, or brush) around. You can also throw treats to your dog while he stays calm and relaxed. Start with tiny movements (a few inches) and build up the movement slowly.

The next step really needs a second person to help. Get the other person to move the hoover back and forth across the room from you and your dog, still switched off, while you feed your dog yummy treats. Gradually allow the hoover to get closer and closer but remember to watch your dog and immediately back off again if there is any sign of unease.

Now turn the hoover on briefly while you feed treats.

You may need to turn it on in another room at first until your dog can cope. Make sure you stop feeding treats as soon as the hoover is turned off - your aim is to associate the sound and movement of the hoover with treats.

Repeat this step, briefly switching the hoover on in the same room while you feed yummy treats. Gradually build up the time the hoover is switched on. Then add movement - just a tiny push at first. Then a bit more. Then a bit more.

Keep practising, until eventually you can hoover with impunity while your pooch enjoys tasty treats or a yummy Kong on his bed.

The same process needs to be repeated with each item your dog is fearful of.

Sandra solved her problem initially by putting Benji out in her garden with a filled Kong or two before she started all her cleaning (luckily it was the summer). She also spent many weeks gradually teaching Benji to ignore and cope with the hoover, then with mops and brushes, until eventually she was able to clean while Benji happily stayed in another room with his Kongs.

Summary

- Most dogs, if not introduced to them as puppies, are afraid or vacuum cleaners and may attack brushes and mops
- You can manage the situation by keeping your dog well away from any cleaning activities

- Desensitising your dog to hoovers, brushes and mops can take a long time and needs loads of patience

There's a lot to digest in this chapter. Talking of digesting, the next few chapters are all about food. Whether it's that your dog won't eat, or is obsessed with finding food, or is a begging machine, you'll find something to help in the next section.

10

HELP! MY DOG WON'T EAT HER FOOD

illy was refusing to eat her kibble. The cockapoo puppy's owners, Laura and Steve, were worried about her. They tried to tempt her by feeding her by hand, but Tilly wouldn't eat one morsel. Laura was convinced she would starve. A young puppy needs her food. Tilly had always been a fussy eater, right from the day they got her. Laura and Steve had tried 3 or 4 different types of kibble over the 8 weeks they'd owned Tilly. Tilly would try one or two bits then refuse to eat. So Laura and Steve added wet food to the kibble. Tilly still wouldn't eat. They started adding some tasty extras to Tilly's food, things like bits of ham and pieces of chicken. At first they fed her cheap Asda value chicken, but even this escalated. By the time I became involved, Tilly would only eat M & S chicken and the Laura and Steve were becoming desperate.

Do you get frustrated and worried because your pooch won't eat his food?

It's one of the commonest concerns my clients have.

You're programmed to care for and nurture your dependents, whether they're children, dogs, cats, hamsters or goldfish. And that involves feeding them. If they don't eat, you worry. Food is, after all, essential for life. You try to tempt them with new or different foods, desperate to find something they'll eat.

Did your mum bribe you to eat your vegetables by saying you'd only get pudding if you ate all your dinner? Mine did. Perhaps you reach for the chocolate when you're feeling low?

Food is very emotive and it's not surprising owners are concerned about what their dog eats (or doesn't).

It's unrealistic to expect everyone (and every dog) to like every food. Himself is a fussy eater with vegetables. He only eats peas, green beans, and sweetcorn. It's a bit limiting. I don't like butter beans, but I love all other vegetables. What about you?

Most dogs eat what they're given quite happily. Labradors are well known for generally being greedy dogs and eat all the food they're offered - and lots of other things too. As can many individuals of other breeds of course - I'm not breedist. These dogs will eat anything they're given, plus begging for anything you eat or stealing any food left lying around.

BHW: Make sure you learn what foods are poisonous to dogs. Common ones are chocolate, coffee, onions and grapes and their dried counterparts. See my website, www.downdog.co.uk to download a free help sheet listing all the foods poisonous to dogs

Some dogs may not like particular dog foods, but will

happily eat a different variety. But other dogs, often the smaller, companion breeds, can be fussy eaters.

You can make a puppy a fussy eater through what you do.

Leaving food down in a bowl so it's always freely available can encourage dogs to be picky about eating.

If you hover by your puppy and show that you're anxious about what they eat (or don't eat), then some pups will use that to their advantage. They'll pick at the food if that gets them more of your attention.

If you add nice human food titbits to their dinner, to try to tempt them to eat, they'll learn to hold out for something better.

And some people just think their dogs should eat more than the dog actually needs.

You care about what and whether your dog eats. Dogs understand this and some will use our emotional need to feed them properly to their own advantage.

Tilly was holding her owners to ransom over food. Because she was always offered something nicer than kibble, she'd learnt to refuse the kibble so she got the tasty stuff instead. And she'd learnt that if she only picked at that she might get something even better.

She'd trained her owners to provide high quality chicken.

Can dogs be allergic to foods?

They can. Around 10% of all allergies in dogs are food related. In an allergic reaction the dog has an immunological reaction to a food or food component. The allergy builds over time and can take years to become evident.

The most common symptom of food allergy is itchy skin. There are, of course, lots of other reasons your dog might have itchy skin, but around 20% of itching or scratching is due to food allergy.

Other symptoms a food allergic dog might show include regular (2-3 times a year) or chronic ear infections and gastro-intestinal problems such as vomiting, chronic diarrhoea or an itchy bottom. Frequent foot licking might also be a sign.

Most dogs with food allergy have a genetic predisposition. Receiving antibiotics early in life may be a factor.

Certain breeds are more prone to food allergies, such as cocker spaniels, German Shepherds, retrievers and dachshunds. It's also seen quite often in Boxers, Springer Spaniels, collies, Dalmatians, Lhasa Apsos, Miniature Schnauzers, Shar Peis, Soft-coated Wheaten Terriers and West Highland White Terriers.

The most common allergens, in order, are: beef, dairy, wheat, egg, chicken, lamb/mutton, soy, pork and, rarely, rabbit and fish.

Dogs are often allergic to more than one food. Soy can cause a range of other health issues too, including reproductive and growth problems, thyroid problems and liver disease.

Treatment involves avoiding giving the dog the food(s)

causing the allergy. Vet diagnosis and supervision is essential.

Dogs can also suffer from food intolerances. Lactose intolerance is the most common form and gluten sensitivity has been seen in Irish Setters.

The symptoms of food intolerance are always gastrointestinal and include flatulence, diarrhoea, vomiting, loss of appetite, weight loss and abdominal pain and discomfort.

Food intolerance is often preceded by a sudden change in diet and may be related to food additives, colourings, spices and preservatives.

Always consult your vet if you think your dog may have a problem rather than trying to manipulate your dog's diet yourself. It's too easy to unbalance the diet.

BHW: *Never try to diagnose or manage a suspected food allergy or intolerance yourself. Get advice and support from your vet.*

But Tilly didn't have a food allergy or food intolerance.

What can you do about a fussy eater?

An important fact: No dog will starve itself if there is food available.

Honestly, they won't. If they don't eat for a day or two, or even longer, don't worry. They're just not hungry enough. Once they *are* hungry enough, they'll eat.

If you've got a fussy or picky eater, here's a few things you can try.

Tip 1: If your pup is a fussy eater, by all means try a

different, higher quality kibble. It's always best to feed the finest quality food you can afford. Check the ingredients list. As with humans, shorter lists are better and you should recognise all the ingredients listed.

If you've been using a cereal based food, try a potato based one.

Or try a different flavour such as lamb instead of chicken.

BHW: When changing your dog's food, always do it over five days to minimise the risk of gastrointestinal disturbances by substituting 1/5 of the food each day.

Tip 2: Make food more interesting by feeding your dog through food puzzle toys, kibble balls, or Kongs rather than in her bowl. Or feed by scattering food on the carpet, or hide small piles of her dinner around your house or garden for your dog to sniff out. Try laying food trails, by putting a piece of kibble down every 20 centimetres or so, for your dog to follow.

Tip 3: Feed your dog by hand as you train her. Using her food as rewards when training encourages most dogs to eat plain kibble quite happily. And your dog will benefit from the training, too, of course.

Tip 4: Carefully measure out the correct amount of food your dog should have each day. If you don't, it's far too easy to overfeed, which will make greedy dogs fat, or, conversely, it'll make you worry about whether your fussy eater is eating enough if there's food left over.

If you feed your dog in a bowl, put the bowl down for 15 minutes then take it up again until the next mealtime, even if the meal has not been finished. Leaving food down all the time will encourage your dog to pick at it and graze, rather than eating it as a meal.

Tip 5: For really fussy eaters, you can try adding a little warm water or watery gravy to your dog's kibble to make it more palatable. Or mixing in just a little wet food may tempt a fussy eater. Just make sure the kibble is the main food your dog gets and beware her using food as emotional blackmail.

And stop giving any other treats.

Tip 6: If your dog has itchy skin and scratches a lot, or if she has regular gastrointestinal symptoms, it's best to get her checked by your vet just in case she has a food allergy or food intolerance.

Tip 7: Wait it out. Be strong.

Apart from not appearing to eat, Tilly was completely fit and well.

I advised Laura and Steve to take a hard line. Stop giving the chicken and just offer kibble.

After five days, Tilly's owners contacted me, worried because she wasn't eating the kibble at all. But she was still full of energy.

I implored them to be firm.

On the 6th day, Tilly ate a few bits of kibble. Hurrah!

Most dogs will start eating kibble after a couple of days, so I was surprised Tilly had held out for so long. I then found out that Tilly had still been given peanut butter by Laura as a treat every evening. No wonder she wasn't eating the kibble. Peanut butter is high in calories so Tilly was getting a substantial proportion of her daily requirements from it.

We stopped the peanut butter too.

And things have continued to improve since.

Summary

- No dog will starve itself if there is food available
- Fussy eaters may be holding you to ransom to influence how and what you feed them
- If you're worried about your dog not eating properly, or if you're concerned she may have a food allergy or intolerance, please consult your vet

Dogs eating too much or eating the wrong things is another common problem, so let's look at scavenging in the next chapter. You may want to avoid reading it if you're eating your dinner though...

11

HOW CAN I STOP MY DOG SCAVENGING?

C hief was excited. His owner, Dave, was showing all the signs of getting ready to go out. Chief hoped they were going to the park again today. Yesterday he'd spent a lovely few minutes eating all the duck poo from near the pond until a purple-faced Dave had arrived, grabbed his collar and dragged him away. But Chief had found other delights on the way home - a discarded cake wrapper under a bush; a few dropped chips with tasty curry sauce; and bonus of bonuses, some horse poo by the side of the road. As they got home, Chief wanted to show Dave how much he had enjoyed their walk, so he jumped up and tried to lick Dave's face. Poor Chief was upset that Dave didn't appreciate his show of love and affection.

Poor Dave. His walks with Chief were a nightmare. Dave had to watch Chief like a hawk to try and stop him eating anything and everything. It was tiring and walks weren't the relaxing stroll Dave hoped they would be. But no matter how diligently Dave watched Chief, Chief kept looking for things to eat and always managed to find something to snaffle.

Why do dogs scavenge?

Dogs are scavengers by nature. Wild dogs became successful through their scavenging habits. Our domestic dogs still have that drive and mindset, to a greater or lesser extent.

Scavenging is a strong instinct in some pet dogs. For some dogs, like Chief, scavenging is irresistible. In their little doggy minds, discarded food and animal droppings can be the difference between life and death. It never occurs to them that the stuff they scavenge could be toxic or dangerous. Food is food - even when it's poisonous to them.

Can you list all the foods we eat that are poisonous to dogs? You need to know...

There are many, but the most ubiquitous are: onions (raw and cooked), garlic, chocolate, grapes and their dried varieties (raisins, sultanas and currants), caffeine (from coffee beans or tea bags), macadamia nuts and corn on the cob.

Blue cheeses pose a danger and fruit pips and stones are nearly all poisonous to dogs.

Xylitol is an artificial sweetener which is highly toxic to dogs. It's increasingly found in sugar-free, diet and diabetic human foods, and some peanut butters.

Finally, mouldy food, including bread, nuts and dairy products, contains nasty toxins.

If your dog eats anything from this list, please contact your vet as soon as possible as even a tiny amount can make your dog dangerously ill.

BHW: Download a full list of foods poisonous to dogs from my website, www.downdog.co.uk.

Around 10% of dog poisoning cases occur outside the home, usually from dogs eating things they find lying around. There's a small but significant mortality rate - around 1-2% of poisoned pets die.

There's been an increase in poisoning cases near me over the past few years, several as a result of deranged individuals leaving poisoned food in public places for dogs to scavenge and eat. I can't imagine why they do it. It's loathsome.

One of the other dangers to dogs from scavenging is from the plastic wrappers and other non-digestible substances that are often consumed along with the food. Small stones are often high on that list. Vet care can be eye wateringly expensive if your dog needs emergency surgery to unblock his intestines after a scavenging spree.

My first dog, Ben, was a food thief. One day soon after we got him, I'd left him shut in the kitchen while I went to work as usual. I'd taken some fish fillets out of the freezer to thaw while I was out, planning to cook them for our tea. I'd left them in a shallow dish, still in their plastic wrapper, on the work surface.

I was gob-smacked when I got home to find the dish

exactly where I'd put it, with the plastic wrapper carefully prised open and still in the dish, but no fish. At first, I thought Himself must have eaten it for his lunch - though that thought didn't last long as Himself has never been known to take the initiative to cook anything in the 40 years I've known him.

Ben had managed to climb on the kitchen stool, place his paws on the work surface and tear open the packaging to get at, and eat, the fish, then get down again without knocking the dish or the stool over. I must admit I was secretly in awe of his thieving prowess. And relieved he didn't eat the plastic. But it taught me not to leave any food out again, ever.

BHW: Plastic, stones and socks are the commonest causes of intestinal blockage in dogs. Elastic bands can be particularly dangerous as they can loop round parts of the bowel and cut off the blood supply.

Dogs will also scavenge poo. All sorts of poo, though horse, cow and bird droppings are the usual favourites. Along with other dogs' poo. Discarded nappies are a special delight to a scavenging mutt. Poo does have some nutrient value from undigested food remnants, so there is a purpose to this revolting behaviour, no matter how disgusting a habit it seems to us.

But, you say, surely my dog must find the taste of the horrid things he eats unpleasant? Well, perhaps not. Dogs have fewer taste buds than we do, so disgusting stuff probably doesn't taste as bad to them as we imagine. But it is unpleasant to you, not least from food poisoning that can produce vomiting and diarrhoea in your dearly beloved canine companions, usually at night and always on your favourite carpet.

Dogs scavenge mainly because it's a natural behaviour to them. But boredom can also encourage scavenging. A bored pooch will follow the smell of food and will try to reach the source of the tempting scent even in the home. Wrap any food remains (and nappies) up well before discarding them in a bin and keep all bins firmly closed and out of reach of your dog.

What can I do to stop my dog scavenging?

The main plank of prevention is owner vigilance. You need to look for possible dangers wherever and whenever you go out with your dog so that you can prevent him starting to scavenge.

Here's some tips to help:

Tip 1: Learn to spot your dog's body language as he focuses in on that discarded sandwich, so that you can interrupt him and call him away. Of course, you first need to teach your dog to come away from things he finds interesting. Here's a brief outline of how to do it:

- Start at home by calling him away from things that are boring for him. Start with something like a house brick then slowly introduce other inanimate things.

- Gradually make it more difficult by calling him away from increasingly enticing things until he will come away from the object of his interest every time you call him. Aim for at least 95% success - that he comes rushing straight to you 19 times out of every 20 times you call him.

- Make sure you reward him responding and coming to you with huge praise and something really good, such as a favourite toy or a special treat.

Tip 2: Keep him on lead as you walk past the pond with its smorgasbord of duck poo. A lead is such a useful tool to limit where your dog can go and it makes it so much easier to keep an eye on what he's doing.

Tip 3: Consider walking your dog soon after his mealtimes, when he's likely to be less hungry and therefore less likely to scavenge. It won't stop the behaviour, but it might help a bit.

Tip 4: Use treats to distract your dog and keep his focus on you when you're out and about. Make yourself fun. Practice your training exercises on your walks to keep his mind away from thoughts of scavenging and keep the flow of treats frequent enough to satisfy any food cravings.

Tip 5: Encourage your dog to become obsessive about playing with you. Use whatever type of game he loves - ball games, tug games, chase games. Keep him focused on that rather than giving him the time and space to think about going off scavenging.

Tip 6: Teach your dog to 'leave it' (that is, don't even touch it in the first place). Here's how:

- Using one piece of food on your fingers, hold at your dog's nose level. If he tries to get it, close your fingers (tuck your thumb in). Keep your hand still. Imagine a piece of elastic between your fingers and your dog's nose. Close your fingers if he moves towards the food, open them as he moves away. As soon as he looks up at you, or backs away from your hand, open your fingers, praise him well and give him a treat from your other hand. Remember to give lots of praise to your clever dog. Add the cue "leave it" once he gets the idea of the game.

- Build on this training by putting a piece of food on your knee, covering it with your hand when necessary, then on the floor, covering it when necessary with your foot, praising your dog and rewarding him with treats from your hand when he ignores the food and stops trying to get it. (An important tip here - don't use a soft food like ham, sausage or cheese - it'll stick to your shoe. Voice of experience talking here...)

- You can then use 'leave it' to mean 'you cannot have that' whenever you need to – discarded food, poo, your rubbish bin, the biscuit on the coffee table, or your lunchtime sandwich.

Tip 7: Satisfy your dog's scavenging urge by providing scavenging games at home. Scatter his food on the lawn, or hide small piles of it around the house. Hide filled Kongs and chews for him to find.

But even these tips might not be enough to stop really determined scavengers.

Use a muzzle if you need to

If your dog is a scavenging fanatic make sure he wears a muzzle when out on walks, especially when he's off lead, to stop him scavenging. It needs to be a basket type muzzle - the fabric ones don't allow your dog to pant or breathe fully and can cause your dog to overheat. You'll find a help sheet on how to muzzle train your dog on my website.

Even with a muzzle, you must stay vigilant. Some dogs will squish the muzzle into soft food or poo in order to lick the goodies through the muzzle. Unpleasant to us in the extreme - especially when we then have to clean the muzzle.

You may not want to use a muzzle because you're worried that people will think your loving pooch is aggressive. Listen to me - it doesn't matter what other people think.

If you need to use it, use one. Your dog's safety is far more important than a few funny looks from strangers.

Dave decided to train Chief to wear a muzzle so that he could still be off lead to run around. He also trained a really good 'leave' cue, so that he could call Chief away from suspicious piles of gung. But he still needed to keep Chief on lead near the pond – the duck poo was just irresistible.

Summary

- Dogs are scavengers by nature and it's a strong instinct in some pet dogs
- Many foods are poisonous and your dog can pick up contaminants like plastic and stones as well, so be vigilant and prevent your dog eating things he shouldn't

- Teach your dog strong "leave" and "come away" cues
- Use a basket type muzzle if you need to

But there's something else dogs will often eat when they're out and about. Next, we'll look at why dogs eat grass and whether it's a problem or not.

12

SHOULD I STOP MY DOG EATING GRASS?

E agerly, Renzo the Labrador set off on his scent track. He was doing really well, moving carefully along, following the human scent. But then he got waylaid - the lure of the succulent greenery nearby became too much and he veered off the track to eat grass, much to the annoyance of his owner, Clare. Fred, who's always had dogs, was watching. "You need to stop Renzo doing that", he said, "He'll be sick if he eats grass."

Why do dogs eat grass?

My dog, Gus, eats grass fairly regularly. His preference is for longish, broad leaved grasses. Himself gets all aerated about it, and tries to pull Gus away from his chomping. Himself is terrified that eating grass means Gus might be sick in his precious car. (Himself doesn't care much if Gus is sick in the house, because I clean it up. We have had words.)

Our beloved canine companions are not like cows or sheep of course. They don't *have* to eat grass. Perhaps you've been told (by Fred, who's always had dogs) that dogs are carnivores - that they have to eat meat. They aren't. Dogs are omnivores, which means they can eat a wide variety of foods. Unlike cats, who are "obligate carnivores" which means they HAVE to eat a meat based diet.

Dogs can eat a far greater variety of foods than other pets such as cats or hamsters. Although meat will normally be the main part of your dog's diet, dogs can also get nutrients from grains, fruit and vegetables. These non-meat foods are a valuable source of fibre, vitamins and minerals and are part of most commercial diets for dogs.

Most owners feed human food scraps and treats too. Just feeding your dog with scraps is not really good enough as you are unlikely to give your dog all the nutrition he needs. But odd leftovers are fine, as long as you know what foods you can't feed to dogs, as some human foods are poisonous.

Who hasn't melted at those big, brown eyes gazing up at you as you nibble your cheese sandwich? A tiny bit won't do any harm, but too much, especially of fatty foods such as cheese, are too calorific and can contribute to obesity in your dog - as well as in you.

Anyway, back to eating grass.

Grass eating has been seen in wild dogs as well as pet dogs. It's so common that most researchers consider eating grass is normal dog behaviour. Dogs can eat other plants too, but grass is the most commonly eaten.

But why do they do it? Well, we're not completely sure.

Many owners, including Fred, who's always had dogs, think that dogs eat grass to make themselves sick, when they feel ill. In fact, from surveys, less than 25% of dogs that ate grass subsequently vomited and only 10% showed any signs of being unwell beforehand. So this common belief doesn't hold up as the main reason for dogs to eat grass. Dogs might well eat grass to help settle their digestion, but this is certainly not the main reason they chomp on the lush goodness.

Some people think it might be a sign that your dog is lacking in some nutrient in his diet, especially fibre, but there's no good evidence of this. However, it's always a good idea to buy the best quality food you can afford for your pooch. Complete dog foods are just what they say on the bag. Too many extras, in the form of treats or scraps, may unbalance your dog's diet, which may in turn encourage your dog to eat grass.

Of course, your dog may simply like the taste and/or texture of grass, especially in the spring and summer when sugar levels in grass are high. Dogs are scavengers by nature so if they find a sweet-smelling clump of greenery they may well decide to partake of a morsel or two.

Finally, your dog may eat grass because he's bored or wants your attention. Boredom or wanting your attention is at the root of many of the odd behaviours dogs do - and eating grass is no different.

What should I do about it?

Eating grass is not something to be particularly worried about if your dog indulges. So if it doesn't bother you and it's not making your dog vomit over your plush car upholstery or on your new carpet, then leave well alone.

BHW: You must be sure that the grass your dog munches on has not been treated with chemical fertilisers or weed killers, which could be potentially deadly for your dog to consume.

But if your dog is one of the significant minority that tend to eat grass then vomit, you may want to do something about it.

Tip 1: You could distract your dog onto something more interesting, such as a fun toy and play with you.

Tip 2: Or simply keep your dog on lead and move him away from those tempting tufts.

Tip 3: Teach your dog useful cues such as "leave it" and "come away". (To see how to teach these, look back at the previous chapter.)

Ask yourself: when your pooch eats grass, what do you do? Does he get your attention by doing it? Gus certainly gets Himself's attention by eating grass.

Tip 4: If attention is the reward he seeks, then giving him more attention on walks by interacting with him more and playing games with him. Doing small bits of training during your walks could also help to solve the problem.

Does your dog have a fairly boring life? The highlights of your dog's day are probably their walks (which may be 1-2 hours at most) and eating their meals (perhaps 5-60 seconds.) That leaves the bulk of their waking day, of 6-8 hours, with nothing much for them to do.

There are several simple ways of making your dog's life more interesting.

Tip 5: Ditch that bowl! Try giving your dog activity outlets such as food toys or filled Kongs to munch on, food trails to follow or food stashes to find, instead of feeding in a bowl. Keep some of their dinner aside and use it as rewards for training.

Training needn't be a drain on your time, either.

Just three minutes doing three repetitions of an exercise three times a day will give your pooch some much needed regular mental exercise. You can fit that into your day in all sorts of ways - while the kettle's boiling for your hot drink; during advert and programme breaks on TV; during work breaks; after meals; or while you're waiting for your cup of tea to cool enough so you can drink it.

Keep life interesting for your pooch and he'll be less likely to do all sorts of things you may not want him to - including eating grass.

By the way, we worked on keeping Renzo's attention on his scent track by moving him away from the longer grass and making it more fun with more toy play - but it's still a work in progress. Renzo just loves nibbling grass.

Summary

- Eating grass is normal dog behaviour

- Distract your dog away from eating grass if you want to, onto playing with you with a favourite toy
- If boredom might be the cause, give your dog some boredom busting activities

Eating grass may not be too much of a problem habit – but stealing food can be. We'll talk about looting louts in the next chapter.

13

HOW CAN I STOP MY DOG STEALING FOOD?

A few years ago, we were on a canal holiday. We were having bacon butties for lunch. Himself decided to go and fetch a magazine from the rear cabin, so put his half-eaten bacon sandwich onto the floor (on a plate of course) and tootled off down the boat. Now our dog at that time, Bryn, had a reliable 'leave it' cue. He got up, looked at the sandwich, then looked at me. Had I said "leave it" he would have ignored it. But I waited to see what would happen (naughty Carol). Bryn looked at the sandwich again, looked at me, then looked down the boat. You could actually see him thinking "no, I'm pretty sure no-one said 'leave it'..." - so then he walked over to the sandwich, paused once more to look at me - then ate it. Himself was not amused.

I've had a few clients recently complaining about their dogs stealing food.

One reported with great indignation the shock and disbelief they felt when the sandwich they had just made disappeared from the kitchen counter in the second they turned away. When she looked down she saw her dog licking the remnants of ham and bread from his lips.

Another client was becoming annoyed and frustrated with her dog. "I can't even put my biscuit down for a second on the coffee table. He snatches it from right under my nose!"

My third client raged about her dog's irritating habit of jumping up onto the dining room table to eat the left-overs from her children's plates after their meal.

A fourth client was horrified when his dog snatched food straight out of his 6 year-old son's hand. He begged me for immediate help.

Of course I'll help - but I have some bad news.

Once your dog has found something tasty on a kitchen counter I can guarantee they'll keep checking there again and again, just in case there's more food to be found.

Once he's successfully snatched that biscuit from the coffee table, he'll become a proficient thief.

Once he's discovered he can jump on the table and find food remnants on discarded plates, he'll keep trying to perform that pre-wash again and again.

Once he's found out he's able to steal food right out of your child's hand, he'll become a consummate pickpocket.

BHW: Dogs have no morals, so expecting them to understand what food is theirs and what is ours is unreasonable.

Why do dogs steal our food?

Dogs who jump up on the kitchen counter, snaffling anything they can find, are a common problem. We trainers call this bad behaviour counter-surfing (or table-surfing).

It's one of the more difficult habits to deal with, since your dog experiences a huge reward every time he steals food: he gets to eat it. And for most dogs that's one of the best rewards they can ever get.

Dogs evolved to be scavengers par excellence and will still scavenge given half a chance. Stealing food from kitchen counters, tables and even directly out of your hands is just another form of scavenging.

Food left lying around is considered fair game by all dogs.

Have you ever watched dogs interact with one another around food?

If one dog is guarding or hovering over a bone, other dogs recognise it's unsafe to approach the chew. But as soon as the first dog walks away or disengages from the bone, it signals to other dogs nearby that the food no longer belongs to that specific dog and the others will vie for the right to take possession of it.

A dog is less likely to grab food off the counter when a human is next to the food, probably because he considers the food to be in the human's possession at that moment.

But as soon as food is left unattended, he'll see that food as available to him with nothing to stop him getting it. He'll have no compunction about jumping up to get it, then gulping it down.

Some dogs will even be bold enough to snatch food out of a child's hand, as happened with my fourth client. This is usually a behaviour that the dog has learned from the child herself. The typical scenario is the child has a food item they didn't particularly like or want, such as a celery stick or bread soldier, and decided to get rid of it by giving it to the dog.

It doesn't take more than one or two repetitions of the child giving the dog food she was holding to make the dog think any food the child holds can be his. So he'll steal it - directly from their hand.

So how do I stop my dog stealing food?

For food stealers, prevention is far, far, far better than cure. In fact, it's the only sure-fire method that works. But I'll also give you two things to teach your dog that will help as well.

The easiest way to stop your dog stealing food is to eliminate the opportunity.

Tip 1: Never leave food unattended. Get in the habit of clearing food remnants away as soon as you have finished with them. Tidy away tins and packets you may have used in food preparation as soon as you've finished using them. Keep bins securely shut and out of reach of your pooch.

You may also need to review and change your own habits.

- Rather than leaving the bread in its plastic wrapping at the back of the work surface, put it away in a bread bin.

- If you need to leave food out to defrost, put it in the microwave or in a cold oven.

Tip 2: Prevent your counter-surfing canine from having access to the kitchen. Keep the kitchen door closed. Or use baby gates or barriers to stop your hungry hound getting into the kitchen whenever you're not there to supervise him.

Tip 3: If your open plan house means you can't use baby gates or barriers, then teach your dog to love a crate so you can confine him there when you're not around to stop him stealing food.

Tip 4: If the phone rings when you're eating your sandwich at the coffee table, or chomping on your evening biscuit, take the food with you as you answer the phone. Don't leave it lying unattended to tempt your canine crook.

Tip 5: Encourage your children to eat at a table, for snacks as well as meals. This not only teaches good food manners, but will reduce the risk of them using your dog as a useful food bin if they don't want to eat the yummy broccoli you've given them.

This tip will be even more effective if you shut your dog away in another room or his crate while the children are eating.

An important point here: the whole family needs to be on board for prevention to be successful. There's no point one family member trying to do something that other people are undermining.

The second client's partner was sabotaging any training. The partner always kept the final bit of his biscuit to give to the dog - but he gave the treat by putting it on the edge of the coffee table and letting the dog take it from there. He'd taught the dog to steal food from that coffee table. I had to be unusually tactful about pointing out what had happened in that particular case...

A note about using punishment

Telling your dog off will do nothing - absolutely nothing - to prevent future counter-surfing.

Firstly, the telling-off usually happens far too long after consumption of the feast for your dog to connect the punishment with his stealing the food. Secondly, it will never be enough to counteract the enormous reward of eating the food anyway.

Any punishment is far more likely to make your dog even more sneaky in his procurement planning. He'll just make sure no-one's around when he burgles the goodies.

BHW: Fred, who's always had dogs, might tell you about all sorts of gadgets to 'teach' your dog not to steal food. These can include booby traps, alarms, or even a motion-detector sprinkler. Please don't use them.

These punishment-based methods are dangerous. They can make your dog anxious and they'll damage your relationship with your pooch. They may even cause physical harm to your dog. It's too high a price to pay for a behaviour that can be prevented through simple management and training.

Worse, there's no guarantee any punishment will even work. The occasional, random payoff of getting food will push many committed canines to keep trying again and again, despite nasty things happening.

Instead, manage things. I repeat, prevention is essential.

But there are two things you can teach your dog which will help stop your snaffling scavenger from becoming a practised criminal:

Tip 6: Teach 'leave it', (meaning "you cannot have ...... so ignore it"), a cue that has massive generalisable benefits. Once taught, you can use it whenever your dog starts to look longingly at your biscuit, or drools by the dinner table, and your food will be safe. Refer back to the previous chapter on *How can I stop my dog scavenging* for details of how to teach 'leave it'.

With practice, you can train your dog that food left on a coffee table, or even dropped on the floor, is not his to take. Your snack will be safe.

Tip 7: Train your dog to 'go to bed'. If your pooch is lying quietly on his bed he can't be jumping up at your kitchen counter or table. The 'bed' can be a mat in the corner of the kitchen, or a bed near the dining table.

How to teach it: Start by the mat/bed. Encourage your dog to step onto it. When he does, praise and treat. Take your time over this step. You want him to be lying or sitting on the bed properly before moving on to the next step.

Once he's happily staying on his mat or bed, step away (one step only), praise, and throw a treat to him. Gradually move away further and further, keeping up the praise and frequent treats.

Keep throwing him treats while you work in the kitchen. Throw treats to him while you're sitting eating your meal. Keep to this important rule - if he's on his bed, the treats come, if he moves, the treats stop.

Dogs are sensible creatures. They'll prefer to stay on a bed and get regular treats than trying to jump up at a table on the off chance they might get a reward. Of course, if you're using this method, please don't let anyone feed the dog at the table. He must only ever get scraps on his bed or in his food bowl. I'm talking to you, all the partners of my clients!

The one obvious downside of these methods is that you need to be present to tell your dog to 'leave it' or 'go to bed'. If you can't be around and food is left out on a counter or table, then you must shut your dog away or close him behind baby gates, or in a crate, or in another room.

Dogs have no morals and if given an opportunity to steal food, they'll take it.

Prevention is essential.

Summary

- Once dogs have found food by stealing from a kitchen counter or table, they'll keep on checking there

- Prevention is key - never leave food out where your dog could help himself
- Teaching some basic manners such as 'leave it' and 'go to bed' can help, but will not stop a doggy opportunist if you're not present. You can only train a dog when you're there with him.

Food burgling dogs are a pest, but dogs who shamelessly beg for food can be an even bigger problem, which we'll look at in the next chapter.

14

HOW CAN I STOP MY DOG BEGGING FOR FOOD?

Late at night, lights on to repel the heavy darkness pushing at the windows, I listen to the wind howling around the house. Sitting at my dining table, I start to feel uncomfortable. I know I'm being watched. I check over my shoulder, nothing. I check the windows. Nothing. I nibble my biscuit, thoughtfully. What could possibly be causing this odd, prickling sensation? Have we got ghosts? Has Big Brother finally entered our lives and consciousness? Has the government finally started to spy on us through our myriad of electronics? Is there an alien presence making itself felt? Then I feel a pressure on my leg. I glance down. All I can see are two big, brown eyes staring up at me. Yes, it's Gus, resting his chin oh so casually on my leg in the hope that manna will rain from heaven and he'll get a bit of my biscuit.

Why do dogs beg?

Dogs are opportunists. Their scavenger ancestry comes to the fore whenever there might be the opportunity to find some food. Humans eating provide dogs with great opportunities to beg for food. You'll find it difficult not to respond to those big, brown, adoring eyes, looking at you so imploringly. Surely it won't hurt, you think, if I give him a tiny crumb?

Unfortunately, it will. You may be setting up a habit you don't want.

Puppies are cute and cuddly and it is so, so easy to melt when they gaze adoringly at you - and you give them that last sandwich crust.

Most of us do give our dog bits of food, of course: the last bit of biscuit, or the end of the ice cream cone, or the fatty bits from the meat, or meal remnants.

Many children learn to drop food they don't want to eat on the floor for the dog. And a hungry hound can be helpful hovering under a toddler's high chair to hoover up the inevitable mess.

Why do dogs beg? Dogs beg if it works for them.

Dogs that are never given human food, and who are never fed at the table, never learn to beg. Cyril and Norman, my sister-in-law's vizslas you met in a previous chapter, have never been given any food except in their bowls, so one of their few good manners is that they don't bother begging at the table.

As with so many other doggy behaviours, it's up to you

to decide what's acceptable in your household and what's not.

- A certain client's dog I know will actually jump on the table when the family are eating.

- Himself used to have a red setter who was just the right height to rest his head on the table next to your plate while you ate.

- Some dogs even try to jump or wriggle onto their owners lap while they are eating.

- Many dogs will regularly bat their owners with a paw during mealtimes, just to remind them there is a doggy receptacle waiting there. Most owners respond...

Poor table manners can create hygiene concerns.

Your dog being on the table, resting his head by your plate or sitting on your lap as you eat risks spreading germs and disease. Doggy drool can be particularly unpleasant. Remember Pavlov - dogs will start producing saliva and drooling whenever they expect food.

It's up to you whether you want your dog begging whenever you eat anything, or pestering people around your dining table, but most people wouldn't want any of the behaviours described above.

If you're happy to share your biscuit with your dog when you're sitting on your sofa, or keen to give your dog that last bit of ice cream cone when you're out and about, it's your choice.

Just remember that your dog will try to push those boundaries and might start to beg at the dinner table too.

What can I do about it?

Agree the rules for your family and household - everyone needs to agree and follow them. Right from the start with a new puppy, or how things will be from now on with an older dog.

You need to consider what other members of the family and regular visitors might want or not want. Your dog will behave with visitors in the same way he behaves with you. It's unreasonable to expect dogs to behave differently just because visitors come.

Tip 1: If you don't want your dog to beg when visitors come, make sure no one in your family rewards your dog for begging. Ever. And I mean, no-one. Not even Uncle George who "doesn't mind a dog begging." Your house, your rules.

Even if (especially if) your dog's begging only works once in a blue moon, he'll repeat and escalate things until his behaviour pays off with a rare food reward. In fact, if he only gets a reward rarely his pestering will become far worse than a dog who gets a reward regularly. Dogs do what works.

BHW: It's unfair to allow your dog to beg at table one day then expect him not to the next. Inconsistency is the worst thing you can do in dog training.

Tip 2: You may want your dog to finish up left over food. If so, put it in his bowl rather than give him the scraps at the table. Sweep up the droppings from under your toddler's high chair and put those in his bowl too. Or put the high chair on a special mat and teach your dog that food on the mat can be his, but food elsewhere around the table is not.

Tip 3: I hesitate to mention it because some people may be horrified to hear this, but many dog owners allow their pet to lick clean their plates after a meal. Admission here: I do. It's an individual choice. But if you don't want your dog to beg at the table, you might want to allow the plate cleaning only in the kitchen, rather than by the table.

So what can you to do change things if your dog has already learned to beg at the table and you want him to stop?

No matter how cute or desperate for food your dog looks, consistency is the key to curbing begging.

Tip 4: Be strong. Don't give in to those doleful doggy eyes. The begging will eventually stop if your dog stops getting the reward. But it will take a long, long, long time.

Instead, provide your pooch with an appropriately rewarding alternative food activity, like enjoying his own food toys, food puzzles or chews. Filled Kongs are useful.

Keep a few filled Kongs ready in the fridge or freezer to use when visitors come. Then you'll always have something to hand when you need it.

Mealtimes are often difficult with a dog who's learnt to beg when you're at the dining table. Here's a few tips to help:

Tip 5: A simple solution is to shut the dog away in another room or outside whenever people are eating a meal. The problem with that is our current eating culture. If you've a large family or lots of children around, shutting the dog away each time someone's snacking can be impossible. But it is one solution to stop begging.

Tip 6: Train your dog to sit or lie down by your side. That's what I do with Gus. I don't mind him begging quietly while lying at my side. But I do object to my trousers being soaked in drool if he puts his head on my knee.

To teach him to lie down quietly by the table, first teach your dog to lie down on cue. (How to do that is described in my previous book, *Pesky Puppy to Perfect Pet*.) Then you can cue him to lie down beside you when he thinks about begging. Just remember to reward him for it, with lots of praise and occasional treat and petting rewards.

But if you never want your dog to beg at the table, then rewarding him with food from the table by the table rather defeats the purpose...

Tip 7: Instead, you could teach your dog to go to his bed or a mat or special 'place' while you eat. Start by standing by the 'place'. Encourage your dog to sit or lie down there. When he does, praise and treat. Take your time over this. You want him to be purposefully lying or sitting on the 'place' before taking the training to the next level.

Once he's happily staying on his 'place', give him a long-lasting chew or filled Kong. If he moves off his 'place', remove the chew or Kong. You might even want to tie the chew or Kong to a suitable fixing, such as a radiator pipe, so your dog can't decide to take it elsewhere to chomp.

Keep to this important rule - if he's on his 'place', the fun food toy is there, if he moves, it vanishes.

It's your choice whether to allow your dog to beg or not. Just make your rules and stick to them. And make sure the rest of the family do the same.

Summary

- Dogs are opportunists and will beg if it works
- Agree and stick to the rules for your household, including when visitors come
- Teach your dog to do something else at mealtimes

We've talked about several problems surrounding what dogs take into their mouths. But what goes in, must come out. And it can be eye wateringly unpleasant. Let's delve into the miasma of schoolboy humour smelly farts next.

15

CAN I STOP MY DOG MAKING SUCH AWFUL SMELLS?

A t a training class, the gorgeous Ruby, a bulldog, was producing frequent eye-watering, gag-inducing smells. I immediately moved across the room. The other attendees tried to be surreptitious about moving away from her, though the "no-go" area created became rather obvious. Even Ruby's owner was waving her hands in front of her face, trying to dilute the stench. We enforced a try-not to-breathe zone around Ruby which helped us during the class. But we had to open all the doors and windows after she'd gone.

What causes the stench?

Smellies, farts, flatulence - whatever you call it, dogs sometimes produce the most disgusting smells. Silent but deadly, or loud and proud, they're no laughing matter - especially if you have non-doggy visitors.

All mammals produce digestive gas. Including us. You probably have a few foods that you know will produce unwanted side-effects the following day. I do - a large portion of red meat or too many pulses will do it for me.

But how much flatulence is normal and what can you do about it?

Overweight, obese and sedentary dogs fart more than active, normal weight dogs - I don't know if there are similar findings in humans.

Some breeds fart more than others, especially bulldogs, pugs and boxers. Why? Because these flat-nosed breeds have to take in more air when eating and drinking - and what goes in must come out.

Dogs that bolt their food can have a similar problem, because as they gulp down the luscious morsels, they also take in air. The quicker they eat, the more air they consume alongside the food. And that air has to come out again somewhere.

As well as air that's swallowed, the act of digestion in the gut creates gases that need to be expelled. These gases develop and build up in the large bowel and are expelled as farts.

Diet is the most common cause of excessive and smelly farts. Flatulence can become a significant problem with diets that are poorly digested, or are high in carbohydrates, because these can both cause fermentation in the gut, resulting in pongy smells.

And don't forget about all the 'extras' you feed - dog treats, human food scraps and those tiny bits of biscuit you share with your pooch. The richer the food, in general, the more flatulence it's likely to produce.

Common human foods that cause flatulence in dogs include soybeans (and soya thickeners are found in many dog foods), bread, beans, spicy food, sugary food, high fat foods, fruit, and milk products.

Even if you're the strictest dog owner who never gives in to those doleful, sad eyes boring into yours as you eat your own food and you never, ever give your dog any extras, your dog may still have a flatulence problem. The dog food you give your dog may be to blame.

BHW: Some dog foods appear twice the price (or more) than others. In general you get what you pay for, but the cost difference is always less than it looks because you'll need to feed less of the higher quality foods. Always buy the best food you can afford for your dog.

Some dogs have food intolerance to particular elements of the diet. These will normally show as gastro-intestinal symptoms such as runny poo, excessive flatulence or your dog may show belly discomfort.

Food allergies are not uncommon. If that's the case, your dog might show other symptoms of allergy, such as scratching excessively, licking himself more than usual and he might develop areas of reddened skin.

If you suspect that food allergy or intolerance might be the case with your dog, please consult your vet so they can do the appropriate tests. Don't try to deal with it yourself. You should only try altering your dog's diet under vet supervision.

A sudden change in diet can itself cause excessive flatulence. If you plan to change your dog's food, make sure you do so over several days or so, changing part each day to minimise the chance of digestive upset and other gastrointestinal unpleasantness.

Dogs scavenging things they shouldn't when out and about, such as poo, trash and spoiled food, will commonly result in eye-watering emanations.

Excessive farts can also be caused by illness and diseases, such as inflammatory bowel disease, bacterial overgrowth in the small intestine, irritable bowel syndrome, parasites, pancreatic disease and tumours. In these cases, the excessive farts are usually accompanied by other symptoms, such as diarrhoea, lethargy or weight change. Consult your vet if you're worried.

What can I do about it?

If your dog is contributing to global warming from their farts, what can you do about it?

Tip 1: If your dog is overweight or obese, then do something about it. It's within your control. Restrict what they eat each day so they lose weight. Check with your vet how much to reduce what you feed each day. Losing weight in itself can solve the problem in some dogs.

Tip 2: For some of the flat-nosed breeds and for dogs who bolt their food, giving them food in food puzzle toys, or in a snuffle mat, or in a bowl specially designed to reduce how fast dogs can eat, can really help as these methods reduce how much air these dogs take in as they eat, thus reducing the flatulence.

Try making your own eat-more-slowly bowl by putting a few large stones in the base of the bowl you use to make it more difficult for your dog to inhale their food and make them work harder for it. Scatter-feeding, by scattering their food on suitable surfaces round the house or garden, has the same impact of slowing your dog's eating.

Tip 3: Be careful what table scraps you feed your pooch. Tiny amounts may be fine, but larger amounts can have you reaching for the air freshener later on. Remember that any extras you feed your dog may unbalance their diet, too, so use your common sense and feed any human food scraps only in moderation.

Tip 4: If your dog is otherwise healthy, you can try changing him to a higher quality diet, though I'd always advise checking with your vet first. Dog foods vary tremendously in the make-up, number and quality of the ingredients used in them.

BHW: No food will suit every dog. The website, allaboutdogfood.co.uk, has helpful reviews and details about different dog foods.

In general, when you're checking the list of ingredients of the dog food you're buying, just as with human food, the fewer ingredients the better. Some foods may seem expensive at first glance, but because you'll feed less of the higher quality, more energy-dense expensive food, the difference in cost each day can be far less than it first looks.

Tip 5: If you do decide to change your dog's diet, make sure you make any change gradually, over 5 days, changing one-fifth of the total each day - or the change may cause even more farts, or worse digestive upsets...

Tip 6: Giving your dog more exercise may help with a flatulence problem - research has shown that dogs who exercise more produce less gas. Make sure your dog gets a good walk and run at least once every day.

Tip 7: If smelly farts are an on-going problem, despite you trying some of the above suggestions, you could try giving your dog activated charcoal treats - they can help with flatulence in some dogs.

Tip 8: And obviously, if you think your dog may have an underlying allergy or medical cause for their unsociable wind problem, please consult your vet.

Ruby's flatulence settled down to more normal levels within a day or so - after all, she's a bulldog, so expecting no farts is unrealistic. We decided in her case the stench was probably a result of her eating something she shouldn't have during a walk the previous day. Her owner committed to being more vigilant in future.

Summary

- What dogs have eaten is the usual cause of smelly flatulence
- Higher quality diets can help, but seek veterinary advice before changing what you feed your dog

- Cut out extras, such as treats and scraps, make sure your dog is well exercised and prevent him getting overweight

I think that's enough about food and digestion. In the next section we'll look at the annoying things your pooch might do when out and about, starting with one of the most common unwanted behaviours – pulling on the lead.

16

HOW DO I STOP MY DOG PULLING ON LEAD?

Katie hated taking Juno for a walk. She'd been so happy to get Juno as a cute 8 week-old puppy, and had looked forward to lots of fun, joint walks together as the puppy grew older. But now, a year later, she dreaded the daily walk and had started to resent Juno. She sighed as the spaniel jumped around her, tongue lolling from her mouth, as Katie tried to put her lead on. As soon as the clip was attached Juno ran to the front door, dragging Katie behind her. Katie grappled with the latch and as soon as there was a chink of light round the door jamb, Juno pushed through. Katie grabbed the lead with both hands, fighting to stay upright as she checked she had poo bags, dog treats and her phone before shutting and locking the door. Wrapping the lead around her wrist and using a vice-like death grip, they set off. Katie begged Juno to "walk nicely" but her pleas had no effect. Katie's arms started hurting within the first few hundred yards as she repeatedly dragged

Juno back. She gritted her teeth. Still 40 minutes to go. Surely walking a dog should be enjoyable, not such a trial?

Why does my dog pull?

Dogs who pull make life miserable. Walks with your pooch become trials. Instead of the fun, joint outing they should be, you end up dreading each jaunt and even resenting having to take your dog out.

So why do dogs pull?

Nearly all dogs, even the tiniest Chihuahua, can walk faster than most humans. And your dog naturally wants to get to fun places as quickly as possible. So she pulls on lead.

If dragging you along behind her gets her to the park quicker, or lets her reach that enticing smell over there, or allows her to jump all over the friend you meet, or helps her get to meet the interesting looking dog approaching, then she'll put all her efforts into pulling - and she'll learn to pull more and more.

She pulls because it works for her.

You try lots of different things in a vain attempt to stop her pulling.

You try to hold her back.

You wrap the lead several times around your wrist.

You try using a short lead held with a death grip.

You keep trying to pull her back to you, or to bribe her back with a treat.

You try an extending lead.

You lean back and let her pull you.

Whatever you try, your irritation increases, and your dog's pulling worsens. And you're stuck in a vicious cycle of both of you pulling this way and that, creating frustration for both of you. Walks are unpleasant for you and for your dog.

Can pulling hurt my dog?

Yes. Pulling is dangerous.

It's not just an annoying habit. There's a huge range of health problems that are caused by pulling - to you and your dog.

Our dog's necks are similar to ours. They contain the trachea, oesophagus, thyroid gland, lymph nodes, jugular veins and spinal column nestled together within a relatively small space, all covered by skin. All these elements can be damaged from your dog pulling.

Dog's skin is actually slightly thinner than ours and if they pull, their skin can become damaged and inflamed and they can lose the protective fur from the collar area.

Pressure on the trachea and oesophagus can cause problems like wheezing, coughing and difficulty chewing and swallowing. Pulling can restrict the blood and lymphatic flow to your dog's head resulting in ear and eye problems from raised pressure. Raised intra-ocular (within the eye) pressure can worsen eye conditions such as glaucoma, corneal problems or eye injuries.

There are many glands in your dog's neck including the important thyroid gland. Pulling causes chronic injury to the thyroid which can result in a deficit of thyroid hormone, leading to hypothyroidism.

Pressure on the veins in the neck can restrict blood flow returning to the heart and raises the blood pressure in the head which can result in small blood vessels bursting in the brain.

Constant pulling can also damage the nerves to your dog's front legs, which can result in lameness and numbness. If your dog licks her front paws a lot after walks it could be a sign that she has odd sensation in her front feet which can indicate nerve damage.

Finally, constant pressure on your dog's neck can damage the cervical vertebrae. Pulling can result in damage to the discs cushioning the vertebrae and cause bone spurs to develop, both of which can put pressure on spinal nerves. This may show in your dog as limited head movement or a change in gait.

But that's not all.

Pulling is dangerous to humans too.

Pulling can cause injury and chronic pain, especially to your arms, shoulders and back.

A good hard yank from your dog can tear your rotator cuff, the mix of muscles and tendons that stabilise your shoulder. And that needs months of physio treatment and may need surgery.

Or your dog might pull you over, risking bruising at best, or cuts and scrapes, or even bone fractures.

Gus once pulled Himself over as Himself was trying to hold a crazily aroused Gus who was trying to act a brave hero in response to our neighbour's dog taunting him through a hedge - and the poor man broke a rib. I suffered a lot because of that incident too…

And there's always a risk that your dog might pull you into the road and cause an accident which could have serious consequences for both you and your dog.

How can I stop my dog pulling?

Prevention is of course best. Teach your puppy from the start to walk nicely on lead. But if you already have a pulling pooch, here's some tips to help you.

Tip 1: If you already have a committed puller, or have a large or strong dog, use a headcollar or harness to help you while you're training your dog to walk on a loose lead.

BHW: I hope it goes without saying that choke chains, slip leads and shock collars shouldn't be used. They cause pain, won't help train your dog, and carry a high risk of causing damage or injury.

Always use a head collar or harness if your pulling dog is medium or large sized as there's a high risk of injury to you from being pulled over.

The best headcollars are those that help you with training your dog to walk nicely. I recommend either the Gentle Leader or GenCon head collar. You'll need to take your time to get your dog used to, and happy, wearing it for a day or so before taking them out for a walk. A head collar must feel odd. Some dogs dislike headcollars intensely and will become squirming, manic monsters in a desperate attempt to remove it. If your dog hates a head collar, then the better option may be a harness.

Most dogs will accept harnesses more easily than they will tolerate a head collar. There is a myriad of harnesses available. Most say they will help prevent pulling or advertise themselves as 'no-pull'. But few meet this criterion. So which should you choose?

The best harnesses to use with a dog who pulls are those with both a back clip and a front chest clip. I recommend the Perfect Fit or Mekuti balance harnesses. Harnesses that just have a back clip will still allow your dog to pull.

You should choose a harness with a Y shaped front that fits neatly between the front legs. The ones with a strap or bar going across the chest area may restrict the normal movement of your dog's front legs and shoulders.

Either a harness and a headcollar will immediately give you more control. Then it's up to you to train your pooch to walk nicely on lead without pulling. Our Simply Stop Pulling online course is available through our website, online.downdog.co.uk. Or you can get help from a good local dog trainer or good local training club.

Teaching your dog to walk nicely on a lead is easiest when they're a puppy, but any age, type and size of dog can be taught to walk nicely using a few simple steps.

Tip 2: Be patient. Wait for your dog to be calm before putting her lead on. Teach her to wait calmly by the door before going out. Take your time setting off.

Keeping your dog calm before and at the start of the walk keeps her more relaxed and gives you the best chance of her walking nicely by your side. Excitement and arousal make it almost impossible for your dog *not* to pull.

This was a big part of Juno's problem. She became excited as soon as Katie went to pick up her lead, then this got worse and worse until by the time she went out of the door she was unable to walk nicely because she was so aroused.

Tip 3: Reward your dog for being by your side, anywhere and everywhere. The easiest way to reward is by giving tiny treats frequently. Give the treat by your trouser seam to teach your dog where you want her to be. Don't stint on the treats. And it needs practice. Lots and lots and lots of practice.

Tip 4: Teach her where you want her to walk first in your house, then your garden. If your dog doesn't understand where you want her to walk when she's in familiar surroundings, there's no chance she'll do it on a walk out and about.

Tip 5: Start adding some movement. Take a step sideways or backwards. Encourage your dog to follow you as you move, then reward her well. Make it fun. Practice this for her whole dinner, piece by piece.

Only then try moving forward. Just aim for one or two paces of her walking by your side at first, then release her to play, or have a good sniff. Then call her back, do another few steps sideways or backwards before trying another couple of paces forward. Be patient and make sure you're rewarding her well at your side. It's not going to be easy for either of you, but perseverance will work.

Tip 6: Start all your training in familiar, quiet places such as your garden or local street. Only walk in busier places once your dog is really getting the idea of walking nicely by your side.

Then it's a matter of practice, practice, practice. Everywhere you go.

Even then, your dog may still be tempted to pull at times, so what should you do?

First, think about where and when you go for walks. If some places make your dog so excited that she pulls, then choose different, quieter places to walk. If your usual walk time means there are too many other dogs and people around for her to be able to listen to you and walk nicely, then walk at a different time of day.

There are two main ways to deal with your dog choking as she pulls you towards the next bush she wants to investigate: the 'stop' method or the 'turn and walk' method. Both are aimed at teaching her that pulling won't get her what she wants, but walking nicely on a loose lead will.

Tip 7: (The 'Stop' method.) As your dog starts to move forwards and pulling is imminent, stop and stand still. It's really important to stop BEFORE she reaches the end of the lead. Stand still and just wait for her to acknowledge you. And wait.....and wait. She'll eventually turn and look at you (in puzzlement) and slacken the tension on the lead.

Immediately praise her, encourage her back to you and offer her a treat by your leg. Once she's back by your side, quickly walk on towards the object of her desires.

If your dog is a committed puller, it may take some time to move any distance. But the method works well and quickly if used *consistently* alongside training her to walk on a loose lead using tips 2-6 above.

Tip 8: (The 'Turn and walk' method.) As soon as your dog starts to move forwards and pulling is imminent, immediately turn and walk in the opposite direction. She has to follow – she's attached via your lead. When she catches up with you, praise her well by your leg and give her a treat.

Then turn back and walk in the original direction again on a loose lead towards her desired target. If she pulls again, repeat the turn and walk. You'll probably need to repeat your turn and walk several times before she gets the idea that pulling is not working.

BHW: This method can make you quite dizzy – so please be careful.

With both methods, you're teaching your dog that she can eventually get to the reward she wants, (though perhaps not to roll in the fox poo), but only if she walks on a loose lead.

Both methods work well - but only if used *every single time* she tries to pull. If you ever allow your dog to pull you somewhere, then she'll keep on trying.

The most important requirement? Patience, grasshopper. Training your dog to walk nicely on lead takes time and practice - lots of practice.

We fitted a Perfect Fit harness to Juno. Katie practised diligently teaching Juno to walk by her side around her house and garden using her dinner as treats. Juno picked it up quickly - she loves food. We also taught Juno to stand still to have her harness and lead on then wait calmly by the door instead of charging out. Gradually we introduced short walks in quiet places, building up to busier places. Katie prevented any pulling by using the stop method and Juno quickly realised that pulling was pointless.

Katie still practices the basics at home but now they're having the enjoyable walks Katie dreamed of.

Summary

- Change to using a harness or head collar if your dog pulls to avoid injury or damage to your dog's neck
- Teach your dog where you want her to walk, by your side, by giving her lots of praise and great rewards when she's there
- It needs practice: lots and lots of practice
- Use either the stop, or turn and walk, method to teach her that pulling never pays dividends

Pulling on lead is one of the two most common unwanted behaviours when out and about. Next, we'll look at the other one – not coming back when called.

17

HELP! MY DOG WON'T COME BACK

Vicky felt she would boil over with frustration any minute. She'd let Toto off lead when she got to the common and he'd immediately set off, sniffing and running hither and thither. At first, she'd enjoyed the sight of her dog having fun as she wandered along behind him, but now, half an hour later, she wanted to turn back for home. At the very moment she inhaled ready to call him back, Toto found the most enticing scent ever. Nose to the ground, he set off into the thicket of brambles. She could hear him crashing about, but he was oblivious to her increasingly desperate cries to "Come HERE, Toto!". Vicky wanted to cry. She was going to be late for work again and her manager would not be pleased. Fred, who's always had dogs, wandered past with Ludo. "You need to teach that dog some manners," he scolded.

Why won't my dog come back?

How embarrassing is it when your dog blithely ignores your frantic calls?

Walkers look at you with disdain and other dog owners smile smugly as they parade past with their dogs looking adoring up at them. You just wish the ground would open up and swallow you. Instead, you continue screeching like a fishwife towards your cavorting canine companion who's completely unaware of your increasing exasperation – he's far too busy chasing rabbits, playing with other dogs, or following that interesting scent over the horizon.

There's little that's more irritating than a dog who won't come back when you call.

As you know by now, dogs do the things that get them the rewards they want – and when out and about your dog's likely to find more rewarding things to do than come back to you.

Toto was the most attentive companion you could imagine when at home with Vicky, but out and about she might as well have been a block of wood for all the attention he gave her. At the common, or on the beach, or even in the garden, there were just too many enticing smells, and too many other things to see and do for him to respond to anything Vicky wanted.

There are several things that influence whether your dog comes back when you call or not.

Perhaps the environment you're in may simply be too new or too distracting, providing an overload of alluring smells, tantalisingly tempting bushes, trees and other objects to explore, birds, people walking past, cyclists, joggers, vehicles, children kicking balls, waves on the beach – the list of stuff that has the potential to distract your dog is long and varied. Or if your dog loves meeting and greeting people he may well prefer to engage in that novel interaction rather than to come back to you.

Other dogs are a potent distraction. If your dog's had lots of opportunities to play with other dogs then he'll most likely make a beeline for any other pottering pooch to try to play with them.

BHW: Right from when you get your puppy, make sure playing with you is much more fun than playing with other dogs

But the two most common reasons why your dog won't come back are:

- you've never taught him that coming back is a Good Thing and/or

- you've inadvertently taught him NOT to come back.

The first essential part of a good recall is all about teaching your dog that coming when you call will bring him all sorts of brilliant rewards – treat, praise, fun toy play, a search game – whatever he most loves and desires, every time he responds to your call. (This does require that you know what he loves and wants, of course - his favourite foods, his favourite types of touch, his favourite toys and his favourite games. Test things out with your dog if you're not sure.)

You may get lulled into a false sense of security by your cute, cuddly puppy. Young puppies want to keep close by your side and they make sure they don't go too far away. But you can get a nasty shock when they become bolshy teenagers at around six to eight months old. One day you'll call them smugly, expecting them to come running to you, only to find they look at you, stick up a metaphorical two fingers – and run off.

Setting up a recall habit right from the start is vital.

The second, and most common, reason for your pooch ignoring your call is that you've taught him not to come when you call – or that coming when you call isn't fun. The quickest way to teach him this is only calling him away from his fun when it's time to go – then putting him straight back on lead and going home. Even if you remember to give him a treat when he comes, he'll still make an association between you calling him and his fun stopping.

Or perhaps he's cavorted around for ages and you've become frustrated and cross with him – and you tell him off when he eventually does come back. It's a very human reaction – but it'll teach your dog that coming back is a bad thing to do.

How do I teach my dog to come back?

For once, Fred was right. Teaching your dog to come back is vital. Recall is simple to teach but not necessarily easy. Start by teaching the basics at home then take it out and about, very gradually proofing it against the myriad of distractions out there.

Patience and practice – lots of practice – using the tips below will get you the recall you want. And dogs who can be trusted to come back when you call can have more freedom.

When your dog comes back to you, no matter what he's been doing or how long it took, make sure he knows it's the best thing he's ever done. You may need to count to ten sometimes. But the day you tell him off for coming back slowly is the day your recall will start to crumble.

Tip 1: Decide on what word you're going to use to tell your dog to come to you. If you've been struggling to call your dog back, please change the word you use. If you've used "come", change it to "here" – or any other word you want. Your dog doesn't care which word you use.

Tip 2: Call him in a happy, excited voice. Why should he come if you bark out the order like a sergeant major on a drill square?

Tip 3: Only call your dog when you're almost certain he'll come – set him up for success. If you try to call him when he's gnawing a bone, or eating his dinner, he probably won't come and you're just teaching him to ignore you. Leave him be until he's finished, then call him.

Tip 4: Start by calling your dog to you often around the house, saying his name, followed by your chosen recall word. Call him when he's lying across the room from you; when he's in another room; or when you're walking around.

Set up a recall habit.

Praise him really well as he comes to you – don't wait until he gets there. You want to praise the act of him coming, from the moment he makes the correct decision until he reaches you. Then give him lots of fuss and a great reward.

Reward every recall really well, using a favourite food, or a favourite toy, or a tug game, huge fuss and lots of enthusiasm. It's vital to set up a super-strong association in his doggy brain between him responding to your call and getting a great reward.

Tip 5: Once he's coming immediately, happily and quickly in the house, take your recall practice out into the garden. When you first go out anywhere, give him a chance to sniff around for a few minutes. Then call him. Praise his marvellousness in responding as he comes to you, then give him a favourite reward.

It's important to increase the difficulty of your recall in small steps. You have to build up your recall difficulty slowly, aiming for a high success rate at each 'level' before moving onto to something a little more difficult.

If your dog comes brilliantly everywhere round the house, that's great – but that's only Reception level. Expecting him then to come back at the park when there's children playing, loads of people and dogs around, a football match in the corner and an ice cream van tinkling is like moving straight from starting to read with Janet and John to trying to read War and Peace.

BHW: Set your dog up for success – it's unfair to get cross with him for not coming back when you've not trained him to do so in that particular place or situation.

I recommend using the 19 out of 20 rule to check when your dog's ready for the next level – when your dog comes back 19 times out of 20 quickly, first time of calling, then it's time to move on. From inside the house to out in the garden; from the garden to an empty park; from an empty park to one with people and dogs in the distance; then a little closer; and so on.

Tip 6: When you first go out to try your recall in the big, bad, outside world, use a long line – a ten-metre long lead. Shorter and longer ones are available but that length is best for the majority of dogs. You can make one out of washing line and attach a clip if you're clever enough.

Attach the clip to your dog's collar, then hold the other end, letting the bulk of the line trail on the ground – don't try to keep gathering it up as your dog comes closer or letting it out as your dog moves away. Having it attached gives you the confidence that your dog can't run off into the wide blue yonder, but you can keep practising your recall safe in the knowledge that you can pull your dog back if you ever need to.

Then it's all about practice. Lots and lots of practice. In all the different situations where you'll walk your dog off lead, with all the different distractions you'll face. Use the 19 out of 20 rule to decide when you're ready to stop using the long line.

Tip 6: Whenever you're less than 95 percent sure your dog will come back to you, put him on lead until you're well past the distraction.

At the beach, Gus's recall is really good, but if there's a horse galloping along I always put him on lead, because I'm only around 70 percent sure he'll come back in that particular situation. I'd rather be safe than sorry – and I don't want him to practice not coming back. Or learning to chase horses...

Tip 7: During a walk, do lots of recall practice. Call your dog, reward him, then let him go off exploring again. Whenever you notice your dog checking in with you, take the opportunity to call him and reward him well for coming.

Nine times out of ten, call your dog, reward him - then let him go again.

Set up a recall habit.

Tip 8: When you're approaching a known run-off place, get your dog's attention beforehand and engage him in an exciting game such as tug or 'find it', until you've passed the danger zone.

BHW: Both you and your dog should be having fun practicing recall

If it's fun, your dog will want to come back when you call. Your job is to find what's fun for both of you – then recall's simple. But if you're struggling and your pooch already has a not-coming-back-habit, please get some good professional help to set you back on the right track.

Vicky followed all these steps with Toto. She discovered that Toto's favourite things were chicken or a squeaky tug toy. With lots of regular practice in distracting situations, using the long line initially, and learning which situations were best conquered on lead rather than off, she's now happy and confident that Toto will come back when she calls. Oh - and she's been promoted at work.

Summary

- Change your recall word if your dog has practiced ignoring it
- Make sure your dog always gets rewarded really well when he responds to your call – everywhere, every time
- Be patient - teaching a good recall take lots of time and practice
- Use a long line or lead when you need to

This chapter has given you tips to teach your dog a great recall when you're out and about. But some dogs decide to take themselves off for a walk and explore. Roaming is an annoying and potentially dangerous problem which we'll look at in the next chapter.

18

HOW CAN I STOP MY DOG ROAMING?

J anet adored her Labrador, Hector. He was such a soft, sweet chap most of the time. But he had one deep rooted flaw - he was a consummate escape artist. A door only had to be open half an inch and he was off. He'd worked out how to combat every type of fence Janet had tried. Wooden slatted rails, an upright wood fence, chain link mesh - Janet had tried them all. Hector either battered or dug at a corner or other weak spot until it gave way, or simply clambered over the top. All the neighbours knew him and several times a week a neighbour would appear with Hector in tow, commiserating with Janet about how he'd got out again. But Janet worried that one day Hector might not come home. She was terrified at the thought of him causing an accident, or scaring someone, and dreaded hearing the knock of doom from the dog warden or police.

Why do dogs roam?

Ah, Houdini dogs. You probably know at least one near you. My Facebook feed throws up a lost dog post several times a week. Despite all our strict dog laws, roaming is still a common problem.

Most dogs are curious and want to be active, explore and discover. And a too-low fence, broken gate, or open door or window makes it especially easy for a curious canine to set off exploring. Some dogs seem to focus all their spare energy on finding ways to escape. Others may roam for particular reasons. A few dogs are magicians and seem to be able to get out of any fenced in area, like Hector.

Certain breeds, such as Labradors, Airedales, Beagles and Siberian Huskies, are natural explorers. But even a mixed-breed mutt can have an insatiable desire to see what's beyond their boundary.

There are six main reasons why your dog might roam:
- sex,
- boredom,
- frustration,
- anxiety about being left alone,
- fear, or
- a strong prey drive.

Sex hormones are strong motivators and can drive dogs to find any way possible to escape from confinement, with the goal of trying to ensure their lineage continues and their sexual urges are satisfied.

Dogs become sexually mature from around six months of age. Intact males will roam considerable distances around the neighbourhood searching for the scent of a bitch in heat, while females in heat roam to put themselves out there so a wandering male can find them more easily.

Boredom is a common factor in dogs who escape.

Dogs left at home all day while their owners are at work can get stir-crazy. Imagine how quickly you'd get bored if you were shut alone somewhere without access to magazines, books, radio, TV, or the myriad of technological gadgets without which modern humans can't seem to function.

Bored dogs look for ways to get out so they can find something to do and in the hope of finding some fun company. Your dog might be keen to visit the children next door for a play session, or have a jaunt round the neighbourhood to check what's going on.

Perhaps your dog lives for the brilliant playtimes he has at the dog park.

Left alone at home, with lots of pent-up energy, he'll use his frustration to try to escape to set up his own playdates with doggy friends.

Or perhaps the frustration comes from other sources. Gus hates the dog that lives in the house at the top of our lane with a passion, so if he ever gets out, we know we'll find him running up and down the hedge near the top of the lane, with the other dog on the other side.

There are gaps in that hedge, but both dogs studiously ignore them. It's frustration-based behaviour, but it's unlikely to lead to anything worse - luckily both dogs are far too wary of each other to get too close.

Maybe your dog hates being left alone at home.

You may have noticed that she seems unsettled and nervous when you leave her. As soon as you leave, she tries to escape – your scraped doors are testament to that. The only good news here is that if she does get out she's likely to stay close to home.

Some dogs seem to hate being left in a particular place, especially if it's a small area, such as a utility room or kitchen, and can cause significant damage to themselves or to the fixtures and fittings as they desperately try to get out.

Giving these dogs the run of the house may solve the problem.

Some dogs escape and run away because they're terrified by something that happens, usually a loud noise such as thunder, fireworks or gunshots.

Around one in five pets goes missing for this reason.

BHW: These dogs can be so scared that they cause huge damage to your house and to themselves in trying to escape, breaking windows and doors or knocking down fences. These dogs need urgent behaviour help.

Finally, prey drive - that inbuilt instinct to chase, hunt and kill something. Dogs who get their kicks from chasing cats, or squirrels, or rats, or mice, and who spot their prey through a fence will often do everything in their power to escape and chase the prey they're laser-focused on.

Is it really such a bad problem?

If your Roaming Rover stays on your property there may be no problem - unless the postman or delivery driver is scared by them, of course. But few dogs will stay so close to home. And that presents a whole raft of problems.

For most dogs, the lure of the outside world is too much and if they get out, they'll usually roam well beyond your boundaries.

In rural areas, farmers may shoot first and ask questions afterwards. And you won't have any comeback. They're totally within their rights to protect their stock. If you live near water where there are swans, these too are protected by law, so dogs who worry them also risk getting shot.

Dogs who run away in fear are in panic mode and can't make sensible decisions. They may crash through open windows, run straight through wooden fences or barbed wire and cause themselves significant and possibly life-threatening injury, or they may run into the road and cause an accident. They can also end up a considerable distance away from familiar areas by the time the overwhelming terror subsides.

In more built up areas the volume of traffic and pedestrians plus loose dog means accidents are just waiting to happen. Your doggy deserter may knock a child off their bike, or he might run into the road and cause drivers to swerve. Both of these may end in tragedy, for both the dog and for others.

Your predatory pooch may cause mayhem chasing that cat, or he may even turn his sights onto a child, or pet rabbit, or another dog, if his pecker's up and his prey drive becomes overwhelming.

BHW: *Dogs who chase things get a huge endorphin release from it and this behaviour can quickly become addictive for them so the behaviour can escalate rapidly*

Remember that practice makes perfect. If you have a dog who shows a strong prey drive please seek professional help sooner rather than later.

So, yes. It's important, nay, vital, to stop your dog roaming.

What can you do about it?

As with all unwanted behaviours, the answer is - it depends.

Dogs whose roaming is driven by sexual urges can be helped by a visit to the vet.

Tip 1: Spaying or neutering will reduce your dog's desire to roam, though it can take a few months before sexual hormone levels subside to their new, low level. Most dogs after neutering or spaying eventually become contented homebodies - problem solved. Unless, of course, the roaming which was originally driven by sexual urges has now become a habit.

Bored or frustrated escapees can be helped with more attention and exercise, both physical and mental.

Tip 2: Make sure your doggy delinquent has a good

walk and run for aerobic exercise each day alongside training games, scent games and other mental activities to tire their mind.

Tiring mental activities can include food puzzle toys, stuffed Kongs, hidden treats left around the house, a sand box for digging - anything your dog loves and that will work his brain. Tired dogs can't be bothered exerting the energy needed to find ways to escape.

Tip 3: If you suspect your dog escapes because he hates being left alone, seek professional help to teach him how to cope better with being left in the home. Or consider doggy daycare, a regular dog walker, or even use a dog sitter if you can.

Similarly, if your dog has escaped because he was terrified by a loud noise, that needs dealing with. Book some professional help to guide you how to teach your dog to cope in those situations.

Tip 4: Make sure you train your dog to come back when you call, in all sorts of places and situations. If your dog does get out, at least then you have a good chance of being able to call her back easily.

Check out our Down Dog in-person and online courses and other help options on the website if you need more help with this. There's a good section on teaching recall in my book, *Pesky Puppy to Perfect Pet*, as well as the tips in the previous chapter.

Tip 5: Work out what things your dog loves and make sure it's you that provides them. Encourage your dog to play with you rather than with other dogs at the park.

Interact with him throughout your walk to build a strong relationship.

A dog whose needs are fully met through interactions with you, his owner, has no need to roam.

Janet learnt to manage Hector better. She upped his exercise and gave him loads more mental activities to tire him out, including some intensive recall training. She kept her doors locked and they decided on an 'airlock' system for visitors coming in and out. Hector was never left unsupervised in the garden; or if they might be distracted from watching him, such as when they were gardening or the children were playing outside, Hector was kept on a long tether.

He's a much more contented and relaxed dog now and he's shown no inclination to try and scale their fence for many months.

Summary

- Roaming is highly dangerous for your dog and for others
- Sexually driven roaming can be helped by spaying or neutering
- Make sure you provide all the physical and mental activities your dog needs. Tired, contented dogs have no need to roam.

Perhaps you're smugly thankful that your dog shows no inclination to roam. But dogs don't have to go off of your property to cause havoc. We'll look at the annoying problem of dogs who dig in the next chapter.

19

HOW DO I STOP MY DOG DIGGING HOLES IN MY GARDEN?

Coco was causing a serious rift in their marriage. Brenda and Ian both adored their playful terrier, but Coco was creating a big hole in their relationship - literally. Ian was rightly proud of his beautiful garden, with its well-laid out beds bursting with colour, textures and shape, his manicured lawn and intriguing winding pathways. But since getting Coco nine months ago Ian felt he was at war. Coco loved to dig. And Ian's pristine beds and velvet lawn were suffering. Every time Ian tried to plant some new plants, Coco lasered in, trying to dig them up. It was causing regular arguments between Brenda and Ian - though Coco was completely oblivious to the problems he was causing.

Coco also dug at his own bed and when on their new sofa. Daily, Brenda was frustrated by her lovely new Laura Ashley cushions being scattered across the room. They needed help. Fred, who's always had dogs, told them to squirt water at Coco *whenever he started digging at anything. "That'll teach him not to dig," Fred crowed.*

Why do dogs dig?

Many, many, many years ago, when dogs were semi-wild creatures, they had quite a lot of dangerous enemies, including rodents, spiders, ants, scorpions and snakes.

Dogs developed the habit of digging and scrabbling at a chosen resting place, tunnelling into a patch of long grass, trampling it down, then turning round in circles before settling down. This activity disturbed any nasty stingy, bitey creatures hidden in the area and chased them away, making it safe to lie down there.

Our domesticated pets still show the same behaviour. Gus has a mad 5 or 10 minutes most evenings when he digs and spins frantically in his bed, before finally settling down for a snooze. Even though we don't have any poisonous spiders or scorpions here (and of course St Patrick made sure there aren't any snakes). His brain tells him to do it, so he does.

But there's a second, more subtle, reason dogs scratch at their beds, or your best Axminster carpet, or your new leather sofas.

Dogs don't have many sweat glands but some of the few they do have are in their paws. These glands also give off scent. Digging and scratching at favourite areas adds scent, marking them as belonging to your dog. Which explains why dogs dig more when you introduce a new dog or other pet into the family – your current pooch wants to make it clear to the interlopers that he "owns" particular areas and the newbies should keep away.

Lack of scent also explains why dogs shun the expensive new bedding you bought them as a special treat. It takes time for the new bedding to gain their scent, so many dogs will pull a new cover off their bed, preferring to settle down in the old comfy and smelly bed carcass until the new bedding is scented to their liking.

Digging is a perfectly normal and natural doggy activity - especially for certain breeds.

Some terriers consider digging to be their reason for existing. Terriers are bred to dig down into holes and burrows to find their prey.

Many dogs find certain surfaces, such as sand, almost irresistible and will dig holes simply for the pleasure of doing so. Gareth's dog, Tippi, will dig a hole in my sand arena to roll in then lie down in every Saturday at our training sessions.

Disturbed surfaces act as a digging magnet, which is why Coco regularly dug up the newly planted pots and plants, much to Ian's annoyance.

Dogs also dig for many other reasons:

- They dig when trying to get warm or stay cool - so you may notice your pooch digging more in hot weather, trying to find a cooler spot.

- They may dig to entertain themselves - boredom is a common reason for digging.

- They may dig to bury valued items, especially long-lasting chews such as bones.

- They'll dig when hunting ground-dwelling animals. I

suspect quite a lot of garden digging is prompted by the presence of mice or other tiny creatures in the soil that dogs can smell and hear but we can't.

- Some dogs dig to escape because they can't bear the boredom and anxiety of solitary confinement. Escaping is exceedingly dangerous for your dog's health, as you read in an earlier chapter, and can become a dangerous habit - once your dog has tasted the heady delights of freedom they'll try again - and again - and again - to get out.

You may think your dog will be more content left in your garden when you go out, but, in general, dogs are more settled, and happier, when left in your house. Leaving your dog alone in the garden can create all sorts of digging, barking or reactivity problems.

What can I do about unwanted digging?

You may not want to do anything. Enjoy watching your dog doing what comes naturally. Digging is a harmless, natural behaviour. Though if the claw marks in your new carpet, or rough patches or holes on your sofa, become too much, you may want to act.

I'm sure you won't be surprised to find that I don't recommend Fred's suggestion of squirting your dog with water. First, it may scare your dog and damage your relationship and secondly, some dogs love it and think it's a game. Either way, it won't teach your dog not to dig. Punishment just doesn't work.

Because digging is so innately rewarding for dogs, it can be difficult to stop.

There are two main things you can do - restrict your dog's access to his digging paradise or give him something different to do.

Tip 1: You can restrict your dog's access to the area you want to protect by shutting doors, using baby gates, or moving furniture.

Tip 2: Alternatively, you can distract him away from his digging to something else he can focus on and loves, such as a tug game, or food toy.

In the home, you can shut your dog out of the sitting room to protect your sofa and cushions. When you do go in, take the opportunity to teach your dog to lie on his own bed or a suitable mat instead of clambering all over the furniture.

Brenda decided to keep the sitting room door shut to keep Coco out. Over a few days she was able to teach Coco to lie on a dog bed by the sofa and the family were able to enjoy their home comforts together.

If you want to protect your garden from the attentions of your marauding mutt, first make sure your dog is never left alone in the garden. If he does come out with you, you must supervise his activities at all times. As soon as he starts, or looks like he wants to start, to dig, distract him with a game or a chew toy.

For all sorts of reasons, I don't recommend leaving your dog alone in the garden. Here's just two:

- You're not there to interrupt him if he gets up to digging mischief, and

- He's likely to develop problem behaviours such as barking, howling or escaping.

BHW: *You can't train a dog or deal with any problems that arise if you're not there with him.*

But if you feel you must leave your dog in the garden when you go out, you need to make it more interesting.

Why not teach recreational diggers to become recreational chewers? If your pooch is busying himself with a chew toy or bone, he'll have less interest in your gardening activities and he'll be less likely to dig up all your new plants.

Tip 3: Give him a selection of food puzzles and chew toys full of his dinner for him to focus on.

Tip 4: Make sure he has a cool resting place in the summer and a warm shelter in the winter.

Tip 5: Check before you leave him that he's well exercised (mentally as well as physically) and entertained.

Tip 6: Be sure to fix the fence so he can't dig his Great Escape tunnel.

Tip 7: You can protect special plants with a lattice of wire for them to grow through. Chicken wire laid on or just under the soil surface can prevent some digging - but tends to get in the way of gardening too.

For really determined garden re-designers, choose a location to your liking and teach your dog to dig there.

Tip 8: Build him a digging pit (much like a child's sandpit) in a suitable corner. Line it with plastic, wood or metal sides to keep the contents in. Use a mix of sand and soil to fill it - your soil may be sandy anyway which would be fine, but heavy clay soils tend to be too firm for a fulfilling digging session and need mixing with something lighter.

Bury really exciting things (such as a bone, biscuit, favourite toy or stuffed chew toys) in the new digging pit and encourage your dog to dig for them. After several sessions where he finds something really rewarding, your pooch will discover that the digging pit is a treasure trove where he can find toys for sustenance and entertainment - and the rest of your garden will be safer from his attention.

Ian decided to dig a sandpit for Coco in the corner of the garden near the compost heap. He spent a few weeks taking Coco out there most days and encouraging him to dig for the toys and biscuits he'd buried there. It's been successful - Coco still needs to be monitored closely when there are newly planted pots of plants around, but he loves his digging pit and spends many happy hours there, digging up his treasure.

Summary

- Digging is a normal, natural behaviour for all dogs though some dig much more than others
- Dogs may dig at soft furnishings to make themselves a comfy sleeping area, or to spread their scent on items and areas they feel are theirs
- Providing a digging area for determined garden attackers can save your beloved plants and lawn

Well, that's all for this book, though there'll be lots more in future volumes.

Read on to find more information that will help you if you're struggling with any aspect of your dog's behaviour.

AFTERWORD

I wrote this book to help you understand why dogs do the things they do, why they naturally do things that we humans find annoying or repugnant and to help you deal with any behaviours you dislike in your own dog.

I've blown away a few common and deep-seated myths about 'dominance' and neutering for good.

I've explained why dogs don't see things as good or bad – only whether they produce results that help the dog benefit from something he wants, or prevent him experiencing something he'd prefer to avoid.

You've read about why punishing dogs doesn't change their behaviour - and usually makes things worse.

And I've given you the three-step formula to help you change any behaviour you don't want your dog to do.

This book has covered sixteen common and unwanted behaviours shown by pet dogs: six you might struggle with at home, six related to food, and four common unwanted behaviours when you're out and about.

I've explained why your dog might perform each behaviour and outlined what you can do about it if you're wanting to change unwanted behaviours in your own pooch.

Here's what you'll need to do:

- use the chapter information to help you work out why your dog is doing what they're doing,

- map out your own, clear, three-step plan for success using the tips I've given you for whatever unwanted behaviour you want to address,

- keep it simple and make it easy to do,

- make sure you get your family's support and help,

- and seek professional help if you're struggling.

I'm struggling. How do I find help?

If your dog has a significant or worrying behaviour problem, especially if the problem poses, or may pose, a risk to you, your family, other people, other dogs or other animals, please seek proper, professional help.

Always take your dog to your vet for a thorough check-up first if his or her behaviour changes. Medical problems can often present as a change in behaviour. (There'll be more on medical causes of behaviour problems in another book in this series). Once you know there's nothing medical underlying your dog's behaviour, then seek help.

Make sure your chosen professional is properly qualified to provide your help.

Unfortunately, at the time of writing, there is no overall registration body and no national regulation of the profession. So it can be difficult to find someone you can trust.

BHW: In the UK, anyone who wants to can call themselves a dog behaviourist - Fred probably thinks he's one.

Ask your vet for a recommendation as they'll know of good behaviourists locally.

If you decide to seek help, here are a few things to look out for:

- Do they have a behaviour qualification such as a degree or diploma?

- Do they prefer or require a vet referral?

- Are they fully insured?

- Are they fully registered with a reputable body? Reputable bodies include being Kennel Club Accredited in Behavioural Training, or being a full member of the Association of Pet Behaviour Counsellors. There are other bodies but, as noted above, there is no national register or registration body - yet.

Ask around your dog owning friends, too. They may know someone or have experience of someone they can recommend - personal knowledge is better than just word of mouth.

Any competent behaviourist will make sure they keep abreast of all the different training methods through contact with colleagues, reading, and at seminars and events. They'll always make sure they understand the science behind what they do and will make it their policy to look for the evidence of where the method will work, where it won't work and where we just don't know yet. They can then use the most effective method in each situation.

Ask them about their background and knowledge.

And ask them about the methods they use. Forceful methods are outdated, often cruel, and unnecessary, as are most training "gadgets".

Avoid like the plague anyone who suggests using choke, prong or shock collars on your dog. If you wouldn't use it on yourself, don't use it on your dog.

Be careful using online advice

As you've seen from this book, there are many reasons why dogs do the things they do, and it can be very difficult to know whether the advice you're given is any good or not.

The internet is a wonderful thing and you can look up nearly anything at the touch of a few keyboard strokes, but there is little, if any, quality control of the information a search produces.

Facebook is full of dog groups where people give each other advice, disagreeing and sniping at each other, with everyone claiming their way is the best. (A favourite dog training joke is that if there are two dog trainers talking, there will be at least three opinions about how to train anything).

Asking for dog behaviour advice on such groups is fraught with danger. To give good advice, the advisor needs to ask lots of questions and preferably see you and your dog. Giving and taking advice on the basis of a short post can be downright dangerous.

Engage your brain before following any online advice and ask yourself - does this make sense and fit with what I already know? If it's something new, check the source out first to see if it seems reputable and sound.

NEXT STEPS

Given you've read this far, perhaps you'd like to know more or find some more help about any problems you're facing with your dog? There's a limit as to how much I can include in any book.

Here's some things that will help:

1) Go to the website, www.downdog.co.uk, to download a free booklet: **How To Find Your Dog's Kryptonite.**

You will:

* Discover the FIVE magic rewards your dog will love

* Learn how to ask your dog what they want - so they'll do what you want. Because training is not all about giving food treats.

All delivered to you by t'internet pixies

2) The website, downdog.co.uk, also has a range of free help sheets, newsletters and blog, where you can find information and articles on a variety of topics.

3) Have a look at our online self-study courses at online.downdog.co.uk.

3) Buy my other books from Amazon. They're available in paperback or Kindle versions or you can get them for free through Kindle Unlimited. Search for The Doggy Doctor series.

Here is a brief synopsis of my other books:

Pesky Puppy to Perfect Pet

From considering getting a puppy or new dog through the manic first few weeks, this book is a puppy bible for new owners, covering what to do about those pesky puppy problems as well as the essential socialisation and training you need to do so you'll have the perfect pet you always wanted.

Chaos to Calmish: Diary of a Pesky Puppy's First Year

This is the honest, contemporaneous diary of the first year of Gus's life, to show, warts and all, what life is like day-to-day with a new puppy. It describes the things I did well and explains where I could have done things better. I'm honest about the mistakes I made and how readers can avoid them. And it's got plenty of lovely pictures of my gorgeous Gus.

How to Socialise Your Puppy (or Older Dog)

This book provides easy to follow, practical advice and tips on how to socialise your new pup or new rescue dog, to help them gain vital confidence and become comfortable with the myriad of things they will meet in our crazy, busy, unpredictable world.

Please may I have a puppy?

This book, aimed especially at children aged 6-14, will tell you what you need to know before getting a puppy, how to choose the right puppy, what to do from the day you bring them home and what you need to teach your puppy to be your perfect pet.

Doggy Doctor Surgery Secrets

This book tells my story - about how working as a doctor helped me become a leading dog trainer and behaviourist, The Doggy Doctor and how this makes me uniquely positioned to help others wanting to become dog trainers. In it , I share how my experience in medicine can help people build their knowledge, confidence and skills to become effective, empathetic dog professionals in their own right.

Problem Pooch Book 2: Stressed to Serene

The second book in the Problem Pooch series covers

stress and fear in dogs, looks at eight common fears dogs might face and how to help them cope. The second part of the book covers ten reasons why dogs might howl, whine and bark. I explain the possible reasons why your dog might behave in those ways and give you a range of tips and ideas you can try to change unwanted behaviours in your own dog.

Rescue Dog Rehoming Remedies (Volume 1)

Eleven of the worlds leading dog trainers share their secrets to successfully adopting, training and thriving with a rescue dog. With contributions from Katie Guastapaglia, Dan Alberts, Carol Clark, Tim Jackson, Suzanne Gould, Steven Wylie, Adam Delderfield, Emma Lee, Sarah Bartlett, Karen Boyce and Dominic Hodgson, it's like having your own personal rescue dog trainer in your pocket!

ABOUT THE AUTHOR

As a child, Carol only wanted two things in life – to be a doctor and to have a dog. Denied the latter during childhood, she finally achieved both aims in early adulthood. She worked hard and reached Director level in the NHS but seven reorganisations in eleven years took its toll and she took early retirement. Still with energy to use, she decided to turn her dog training hobby into a proper business. She set up Down Dog Training and Behaviour in 2008, finally retiring in 2022.

She's has been training people and their Perfect Pets for nearly 40 years now (she started young). Getting a dog with various issues and problems made her realise how little she actually knew and resulted in the years of work and study that made her a top accredited trainer and behaviourist.

Carol, The Doggy Doctor, lives in Northern Ireland. She's a Kennel Club Accredited Instructor in Companion Dog Training and in Behavioural Training, is a Qualified International Dog Training Instructor and holds the Advanced Diploma in Canine Behavioural Management. She's passionate about helping people with their Problem Pooches.

But she's not just about dogs. She set up her dog business to help fund her craft and book addictions. She enjoys a range of crafts for relaxation, including card-making (see craftycarolscards.co.uk), bobbin lace and crocheting rugs and toys. She's an avid reader and has far too many books, according to Himself. And that doesn't include the thousands of books on her Kindle account...

A few years ago she started writing her own books which have received many 5 star reviews on Amazon.

Various clients and friends urged her to keep writing more books, so, after much procrastination, endless cups of coffee and a good kick up the rear, more have appeared. And there are more to come...

COMING SOON...

Problem Pooch to Perfect Pet series

Book 3: (title to be finalised)

T his third volume in this series covers medical factors that can lead to behaviour problems and deals with aggression in all its varied forms, including to people and to other dogs.

Doggy Doctor: More Surgery Secrets

More tales from the surgery that have helped me to deal with dog owners and their problem dogs and why dog trainers are actually human trainers.

ACKNOWLEDGMENTS

Writing a book is hard work. No-one can force you to do it. You have to fight through the many days where you can't seem to find two words to link together in the empty cavity of your skull and enjoy the rare occasions when the words trip over themselves to flow out of your crowded brain onto the page.

I couldn't have written this book without the staunch support of several important people. I hope I can do you all justice here.

First thanks to Gareth, my right-hand man in Down Dog. He never realised, when he first brought his puppy to me for training all those years ago, what he'd get himself into. You've also developed into a great dog trainer yourself. It was wonderful watching your confidence build and it has been a privilege to help you gain dog behaviour experience.

Down Dog grew exponentially thanks to pet dog business goo-roo Dom Hodgson, of growyourpetbusinessfast.com. His no-nonsense, straight talking help and support was sometimes hard to take but he never stopped pushing me to develop further. He kept my nose to the grindstone when I was tempted to sit back on my laurels. Thank you Dom. You are great.

Huge thanks to Vicky Fraser of Moxie books at moxiebooks.co.uk. Vicky, you've given me the belief and confidence I needed to write my books - and shedloads of practical help and critiques, too. Your Moxie Books membership group is such a support and without your enthusiasm and constant encouragement I doubt my books would ever be finished. Your brilliant book, *How the Hell do you Write a Book?*, is a writing bible and I'm delighted to be enjoying my publishing journey with you at my side. Heartfelt thanks.

Rob, cartoonist extraordinaire, can be found at everyonelovescartoons.com. His wonderful drawings captured the essence of each topic and make me smile every time. Thanks Rob. I'm glad to be continuing my own cartooning journey with you.

Last but not least, thanks to my long-suffering husband, David aka Himself, who puts up with my tetchiness and frequent computer-related outbursts when things aren't going as I want them to. He does so much in the background to support me, from taking Gus for walks, to arranging his own life around my other commitments. He's always there for me when things are tough. David, you have no idea how much I need and love you. Thank you from the bottom of my heart.

Thanks to all you guys. You rock and I'm so lucky to have you all in my life.

I wouldn't have become The Doggy Doctor without all

the dogs I've had in my life. Each one has taught me valuable and essential lessons - and will continue to do so.

Finally, heartfelt thanks to all my clients. Without you I would not have had such rich stories to illustrate the problems I've described. Despite my anonymisation, you may recognise yourselves in this or in the other books in the series - but I promise I will never tell!

Lightning Source UK Ltd.
Milton Keynes UK
UKHW020639050922
408358UK00009B/994